AF075797

ARRIVED
28 JUN 2007
SYDNEY AIRPORT
4820
AUSTRALIA

NEW ZEALAND
2080
14 AUG 2015

IMMIGRATION OFFICER
5 FEB 2012
HEATHROW

ARGENTINA

"Whether it's 'Poffers' in Perth, or midnight meanders through Antipodean cities, Liam's knack of encapsulating so succinctly the unknown tour diaries of journos on the Bok beat is a joy to read. Perhaps the most delightful thing about *Winging It* is the light-hearted manner in which he encapsulates instances that, with a less socially responsible writer, had the potential to spark a South African social meltdown. That he speaks to the human and ridiculously hilarious aspect of what, in retrospect, are stories that would skirt controversy back home is revealing. Liam is a storyteller through and through ... and his stories are humorous, but above all, stories worth telling."
– **Xola Ntshinga**, former SuperSport anchor

"A great read that gives you a different insight into the rugby landscape. What happens on tour never stays on tour ... offers something fresh when it comes to rugby writing. Finally, a book that will help rugby players realise journalists are also human." – **Owen Nkumane**, former Springbok hooker

"This book reads incredibly well and is so different from the usual stuff that is written in articles or biographies." – **Naas Botha**, former Springbok captain

"Touring the world watching sport may seem all glamorous and highly enticing to those on the outside. However, there are many incredibly challenging aspects that make up the life of a travelling journalist. Liam Del Carme captures all of these beautifully, telling wonderful stories and, most importantly, relating them with great humour in *Winging It*." – **Natalie Germanos**, cricket commentator

"Liam is one of the true rugby gentlemen and one of the most experienced members of the travelling media. His insights into what happens on tour, particularly behind the scenes, are a great read and thoroughly entertaining." – **Joel Stransky**, former Springbok flyhalf

"Rugby is about so much more than just the players on the field, and the media plays a big part in the bigger picture. This book gives insight into their experiences." – **Jean de Villiers**, former Springbok captain

"The adage 'truth is stranger than fiction' has never been more in play as my old SuperSaturday pal Liam Del Carme shares some of his stories of the road. Well travelled, highly respected, eloquent (and conveniently for travel purposes, small of stature) let Liam entertain you." – **Neil Andrews**, SuperSport presenter

WINGING IT

First published by Jacana Media (Pty) Ltd in 2019

10 Orange Street
Sunnyside
Auckland Park 2092
South Africa
+2711 628 3200
www.jacana.co.za

© Liam Del Carme, 2019

All rights reserved.

ISBN 978-1-4314-2913-4

Also available as an ebook.

Cover design by publicide
Editing by Sean Fraser
Proofreading by Joey Kok
Set in Ehrhardt MT Std 11pt/16pt
Printed by ABC Press, Cape Town
Job no. 003638

See a complete list of Jacana titles at www.jacana.co.za

WINGING IT
On tour with the Boks

Liam Del Carme

Contents

Introduction – **Getting off the Ground**	1
Chapter 1 – **Destination Palpitations**	5
Down in Mexico	5
Spitting images	9
Heading for trouble	12
A brief diversion	16
Goodbye, Tintin	18
Almost banged up in Buenos Aires	23
Unsung heroes	26
Chapter 2 – **Planes, Trains and Automobiles**	29
Cleared for take-off	29
Touch-and-go Kai Tak	33
Getting bumped	35
Finding our Chacras	38
Waiting in rain	42
Marooned in Manly	46
Percy and the badger	48
The worst ever	50
Generally speaking	53

Chapter 3 – "No, You Didn't!"	**57**
The Knight of Northbridge	57
Absolute catastrophe	60
A nip in the air	61
Cubana ooh-la-la	62
What's in a name?	63
Loose forward and a hooker	65
Missing "that" try	67
Scrub, scrub, scrub	68
"Please go, Dave!"	71
In the nick of time	72
Enough is enough	76
Some ID please	77
Presidential treatment	79
Chapter 4 – The Poffers	**81**
In from the cold	81
Poffers on a plane	83
Poffers in a lift	85
Poffers off a plane	87
Poffer off a train	89
Poffer at a pillar	90
Chapter 5 – After Midnight	**95**
Late-night craving	95
Back to the scene of the crime	97
"Let me show you Paris"	100
Dancing queens	103
Bring me a bucket	105
A "tight five" go walkabout	107

Dreaded moment	109
Whiskey or whisky?	111
Bobo and Jerry	112

Chapter 6 – **Pressing Matters** — 115

Coaches' quirks	115
Jones jets in fuming	120
Axe the captain	123
"Fatalistic incomprehension'"	127
The Harry moment	130
Fast Eddie	131
Melbourne meltdown	133
Heyneke, it's all about the here (and now)	137
Eye on the prize	138
What's up, Doc?	140
In Jean's words	142
Tales from the pack	144

Chapter 7 – **Being Black** — 147

Shifting tides	147
Darkness falls over the Andes	149
Going bananas	151
Beige suede shoes blues	155
Cementing his place	156
Mistaken, again	157
Chester missing	159
Something stirs in Lake Taupo	161
Lingering tension	166
No snow in Cardiff	168
Filter or plain	169

Chapter 8 – **Being There** — 171

The other World Cup — 171
Indomitable spirit — 176
Going out in song — 178
Nine days in Taupo — 183
Friends and foes — 186
Jannes LabuShame — 188
The venues — 192

Chapter 9 – **It Will Never Be the Same** — 197

Meeting deadlines — 197
Get out of Dodge — 200
Doomed — 204
Buenos Aires calling — 205
Trip them up — 207
Getting to Japan — 211

Epilogue – **Japan and its Wonderfully Wild World Cup** — 215

On the move, even if it's in the wrong direction — 216
Bad company, maybe not — 218
Bokking the trend — 221
Trouble stirring — 223
Boks on course despite the typhoon — 224
They said it — 227
Horrible Hagibis — 229

Acknowledgements — 233

Introduction

Getting off the Ground

THE PUBLISHER'S BRIEF was simple: write a book that places the reader in the shoes, boots of a rugby writer on tour with the Springboks.

There have been a number of books chronicling the highs and lows of Springbok rugby since readmission in 1992 but none, from a writer's perspective, has dealt with the ecstasy and agony of life on tour. This book reflects on my 23 years touring with the Springbok national teams and is also dotted with the experiences of others I've encountered on this journey.

Getting paid to watch rugby and travelling to every continent, except Antarctica, has been humbling and exhilarating. It remains an immense privilege.

In the weeks leading up to a long tour, people often ask, "Can I hide in your bag?", "Do you need a photographer?", "Can I carry your bags?", but the reality is the vicissitudes of touring isn't for everyone.

It certainly isn't as glamorous as it is often made out to be. Sure, if your seat is somewhere near the front of the plane, your upper-floor hotel room has a corner balcony and your road transport is arranged by the concierge desk, then your experience is likely to be more pleasurable.

Touring, particularly the tours that last more than a month, can put you through an emotional ringer. Unexpected news from home or the office can violently alter the course of your trip. I've seen grown men's souls depart their bodies after a call from wife, girlfriend or line manager.

Touring is about rolling with the punches because each day or week brings new challenges. Travelling to cold climes with the Boks invites the risk of illness, which may be a dampener, but it's better to have a cold than, say, haemorrhoids, when you're about to be seated across the Indian Ocean.

Touring is really about taking things in your stride. You can, for instance, get soaked simply because you can't hail a taxi late at night in Paris or because you are one of the thrill-seeking occupants in a jet boat near Lake Taupo, the biggest lake on New Zealand's North Island.

You can jump to conclusions about whether a player is feigning injury, or jump off a bridge in north Auckland with a thick rope reassuringly attached to your ankles. You can lament your fast-diminishing tour-allowance dollars one moment and feel a million bucks the next because of how your latest writing was received.

In the first week, especially if you are in a place you haven't been to before, you may be enthused by new discoveries. In the second week you fall into a workflow rhythm and pattern because by then you've managed to figure out the time difference and how best to meet your deadlines. You spend less time seated as your stomach grows more accustomed to the water the locals drink. The local currency is now also starting to make sense.

In week three you get those tingles of missing home. It is also around this time that some of your fellow scribes on tour start getting under your skin. It may be related to their punctuality while the taxi's meter is running, their hygiene, the way they eat a crab vindaloo, their obsession with one topic or fast food, their devotion to the orange man in the Oval Office and the Bulls.

Ultimately, however, you know that you are all in the same boat. You have a job to do in an environment where the team often resents your very existence and that – that brotherhood with those around you – is often the only thing that keeps you sane.

By week four you feel somewhat numb and potentially impervious to outside influence. Your writing by now is completely unshackled because you have seen enough of this particular incarnation of Springbok rugby to know what's coming. By then it is also abundantly clear that somewhere along the line you have pissed people off. You feel less foreign.

If you're covering a Rugby World Cup (RWC), it is also around this time, in anticipation of the knock-out phases, that fresh faces join the touring scribes. Their rapture at being on tour is usually short-lived, however. After the first or second night on tour they wake up, eventually, feeling they'd rather be caught in the peak-hour entrapments of the William Nicol offramp. Their mouths would be as dry as Cape Town around Christmas 2017. They would have been out the night before with grizzled road warriors who have the momentum of four weeks of touring. Whether it applies to the Boks or the writers, the value of momentum can never be understated.

Even experienced travellers have to keep their wits about them that deep into a tour. Things that may seem obvious aren't necessarily. You may, for instance, have to board a flight from Melbourne to Sydney and arrive at the domestic terminal only to be told you're on an Air China flight and that you need to make your way to the international terminal with only 30 minutes before take-off.

To your relief you discover that a customs officials' strike has resulted in lengthy queues but still you manage to get on board. Your joy is short-lived, however, because you have to occupy a middle seat in the last row of a rust bucket of a 747 that rattles more than the cot of a restless overgrown baby.

You are deprived of much-needed sleep, but you also know that when you touch down, it's time to go again.

The lack of sleep is a constant on tour. Different time zones can wreak havoc with the body clock, while meeting deadlines also brings weight to your eyelids. Often, however, when you do make it to bed insomnia makes for a deeply undesirable bedfellow.

Thankfully, I have found cures in different places. The O Bar in Soho, Downtown Matias in Buenos Aires, the Green Linnet in Paris, Scruffy Murphy's in Sydney, Whistle Binkies in Edinburgh, Sam's in Cardiff, Whelan's in Dublin, The Victory Hotel in Brisbane, Molly Malone's in Wellington, The Gutiérrez in Mendoza, Hula Bula Bar in Perth, Danny Doolan's in Auckland, Box Caffé in Padua and Joe Bananas in Hong Kong all helped me overcome that affliction.

Now come fly with me.

One

Destination Palpitations

Different destinations bring different challenges. Even when you think you know a place, a surprise is never far off, whether it is furthest west on the map, or on the opposite side of the world.

Down in Mexico

THE TRAVELLING CIRCUS that is the World Sevens Series is on the move. It's on to San Diego and this time, thanks to the Springboks' main sponsor Sasol, a few South African journalists have managed to get their passports stamped for the junket.

There is much to look forward to. By the end of the tournament I would have been on assignment with our national rugby teams to every continent. The week is, however, not just about the rugby.

Given San Diego's proximity to the southern border, a quick trip to Tijuana on the Mexican side has its own allure. Fellow hack Brenden Nel (or, as we call him, Baksteen or

Steen, because he once masqueraded as a prop with that name) has suggested we take in Tijuana and a sticker in our passports was supposed to smooth our path. Tijuana has always been portrayed as a gritty border town in which anything goes. Despite the orange man in the White House, it remains the busiest border crossing in the world, a spectacle we are keen to observe.

Our route to San Diego takes us through Washington's Dulles International, where we are to connect for our onward journey to what is then still awkwardly known as Lindbergh Field in San Diego. (Racist and anti-Semitic views have seen the pioneering aviator's legacy nosedive.)

In transit I buy two newspapers. My blood turns cold as I turn to page three of *USA Today*. In the main image headless bodies dangle from a bridge in Tijuana. That's bad enough, but the fact that these are policemen drives home the potential peril we are headed for a few days later.

A month earlier, Mexican president Felipe Calderón had beefed up his war on the city's drug lords by deploying the army. The cartels lashed out, and beheading cops before dangling them from bridges was supposed to convey a certain message.

Still, Steen and I are determined to cross the border. For heaven's sake, we live in Gauteng – nothing scares us, we think.

Our hotel is in San Diego's vibey and architecturally charming Gaslamp Quarter. The streets are lined with restored nineteenth-century buildings that house restaurants, coffee shops, nightclubs and bars.

Steen and I are on the move. We are on foot, trying to shake what we believe is jet lag. It's mid-afternoon and time for a late lunch. At a busy intersection we get the green light, but Steen is rooted to the spot. His gaze is set diagonally to the left and as I'm about to berate him I recognise the sign that has made his jaw drop. There's a Hooters across the street.

"We can have a snack there," I say, pointing in the hope of snapping his trance. He enthusiastically follows as we cross the street.

They say that everything is bigger in America. It's pointless to argue the contrary. The size of those Hooters wings will forever haunt me.

Before the tournament, which is to prove a disappointment for the Blitzbokke, kicks off, we want to venture south of the border. We rather foolishly hail a taxi from the Marriott. Foolish because the 30-kilometre taxi ride is going to cost us a fair bit, but it's going to be quicker than taking the trolley and time is against us.

So we walk into Tijuana but not before meeting the demand of Mexican border officials of $30 each. The visas in our passports apparently mean nothing. On foot there isn't much to see of a part of town that seems to be stuck in the mid-1970s. We see no cops dangling from bridges and in Don Julio (at $6 a shot) we strike a deep and enduring friendship.

We head back but not before a mariachi band stereotypically refuses to take "no" or even "NO!" for an answer. Before we cross the border we are ordered aside by Mexican officials. Routine questions about what we are doing in Mexico follow as well as a body search, which involves us standing facing a wall, legs apart. We cross the border unscathed.

Our hotel is right next to Petco Park where the Sevens tournament is being played so the only other excursion that warrants a taxi ride is to Miramar Air Station, 20 kilometres north of the city.

Miramar was the setting for the 1986 box-office hit *Top Gun*, the movie with a catchy soundtrack in which a hotshot naval aviator (Tom Cruise) takes his instructor's (Kelly McGillis) breath away. Or was it the other way round? We are heading there on invitation from the team who sets off about 45 minutes before we do.

The taxi driver stops well short of the gate. He is reluctant to have his car searched so we get out. Steen explains to a rotund guard why we are there. A liaison officer is supposed to smooth our passage into the base, but isn't immediately available on his mobile phone. We are allowed in and although we are on foot are pointed to a holding area for vehicles, and it is here that Steen establishes contact with our man on the inside.

The liaison officer, however, needs to speak to the guard and Steen needs to hand his phone over to her. Steen, with as much urgency as when he crossed the road to Hooters days earlier, breaks into a trot as he heads back towards the gate. I think his indecent haste bold. Running, or even trotting to the gate of an American air force base, irrespective of the side you are approaching from, is foolhardy, even if five-or-so years have passed since 9/11. Steen would later explain that international roaming costs and his modest salary necessitated his urgency in the moment.

As he rounds the corner of the building from which the officers operate first a firm, then hysterical voice cuts through the air. "STOP! STOP right there. I'm ordering you to stop. STOP! On your knees. On your knees!" I recognise the voice as that of the rotund guard.

By then I have positioned myself to catch a view of what is unfolding. "I'm ordering you to get on your knees," she commands. Steen is trying to get a word in but her booming voice – not to mention the firearm she is pointing at him from about five metres – holds sway. Steen is on his knees and then has to lie face down before he is ordered to let go of his phone. Thankfully, he complies. He tries to explain that he is merely trying to hand over the phone.

Another guard eventually picks up the device and has a short conversation with the liaison officer. Steen is finally ordered to his feet and his phone handed back.

We are allowed to proceed.

As we step out of the vehicle that picked us up at the gate the gravity of what has just happened sinks in. The signs around the base are loud and clear: "Anyone taking photographs without permission will be met with deadly force."

It is not lost on me that we survived Tijuana only for Steen to almost meet deadly force in one of the safest places on the west coast of North America. As 1980s pop idol Kenny Loggins put it in *Top Gun*, this is the "highway to the danger zone".

Spitting images

The last tour on which the Springboks deployed, a midweek or dirt tracker team was in 2000 on their gloriously long tour of Argentina, Ireland, Wales and England.

The first match of the tour is in Tucumán – or San Miguel de Tucumán, as it is officially known – which lies in the foothills of the Andes in northwestern Argentina. It is the capital of the Tucumán province, the second smallest and most densely populated in the country. The topography around the university town reminds me of the area between Wellington and Paarl, with agriculture clearly an important part of the diverse local economy.

The Boks check into a hotel in a decent part of town. Across the road is the impressive Parque 9 de Julio (Ninth of July Park). It's hard to miss and the locals seem to use all it has to offer.

For some reason, however, the biggest men in town seem to be alternating shifts on the gym equipment opposite the entrance of the hotel. Stocky but muscular men, often with lush facial hair, would put their bodies through all kinds of physical endeavour as the sweat dripped from their uncovered chests. The rugby writers aren't quite sure what to make of it, neither do the midweek coaches on that tour Allister Coetzee and Frans Ludeke. Is this what the locals do every day or are they trying to scare the Springbok midweek team ahead of their much-hyped clash against Argentina A?

After all, the Boks have a history here.

On an earlier tour in 1993, the tourists had been involved in a tempestuous match now etched in Springbok folklore as "The Battle of Tucumán" – there had of course been an actual Battle of Tucumán, but that happened in 1812 during the Argentine War of Independence. In the first scrum, in the more modern version of the battle, both sets of forwards suddenly stood up and furiously swung their arms at each other. The second scrum led to more violence and the match was basically marred by flashpoints throughout.

The Bok captain for that match, Tiaan Strauss, later reflected they had to fight fire with fire. And Prop Keith

Andrews would recall how when the Springbok team bus stopped at the stadium, a little boy welcomed them by showing the middle finger. Andrews was later generously spat on by the crowd after he was sent off. Some of the local players and even the coach were heavily sanctioned afterwards.

Surely, I think, that kind of deplorable behaviour would not repeat itself? Besides, the Springboks are playing Argentina A rather than tetchy locals, and referees are now less tolerant of players who resort to violence.

The atmosphere outside the Estadio Monumental President José Fierro is friendly enough, and there is even time for a local version of a boerie roll, or at least that's what it vaguely resembles. The Argentines have a deep and abiding love of meat, so I have no concerns.

Inside the stadium however the mood is very different. As foreigners, you are quickly made to feel unwelcome. The press box doesn't have reserved seats so fellow writer Clinton van der Berg, from the *Sunday Times* at the time, and I slip into one of the empty radio commentary booths.

Estadio Monumental, like most stadiums in Argentina, is an uncomplicated concrete expanse, punctuated by razor wire. Inside it feels cold and inhospitable and it makes sense to have a barrier between us and the general chill. But no sooner have we settled in when we start getting curious stares from the young lads in the back row outside the commentary booths. They are probably in their late teens but are becoming increasingly restive.

Every time Argentina A launches an attack, they – swept up in the moment – jump from their seats, some even banging on the commentary-box window, to look us in the eye. There are a lot more of them than us, so I draw comfort from the fact that Clinton used to be a handy boxer.

All too often Argentina A's advances come to naught and the lads swing around and glare at us as if it were our fault. They have much to shout about in the first half, however. The Bok scrum is in full retreat and the hosts could have been out of sight by halftime. But they aren't and the introduction of Lawrence Sephaka to the Bok scrum, ostensibly to quell the advances of the grizzled Roberto Grau, does the trick. The Boks don't just slip out of reverse gear, and are now marching the locals back – much to the chagrin of the hyped testosterone right in front of us, and the rest of the crowd.

The Boks make a stirring comeback and win 32–21 and so, careful to avoid being spat on, we wait for the crowd to subside before we make our exit.

Heading for trouble

Courtenay Place, from where it intersects Taranaki, is – geographically speaking – the gateway to nocturnal activity in the New Zealand capital, Wellington. The street is lined with restaurants and bars, some of which stay open until dawn, but has the odd cinema and theatre too. The most celebrated is the Embassy Theatre, which stands at the head of the street. This was the venue for the world premiere of *The Lord of the Rings: The Return of the King*, but watching box-office blockbusters hardly features as a "must do" for those who travel that far south.

The pub Molly Malone's guards the top of the street and is usually a good stop to set the tone for the evening. Further down the stretch, however, El Horno beckons. If you can't get into El Horno, then Kitty O'Shea's next door will also get the job done. The locals, including the Hurricanes players, seem to prefer Kitty O'Shea's (renamed Siglo) as it affords them a small measure of privacy upstairs.

El Horno and Kitty O'Shea's are part of a clutch of bars whose doors remain open until 4am, if not later. To get to El Horno, a Hispanic-themed bar, requires a bit of a stroll down Courtenay Place but even in the biting cold we figure it's worth it. It's great for people watching, and the quirky Kiwis never disappoint. You never know who you might bump into. You could, for instance, be minding your own business, just two sips away from heading back to your hotel, when a former Springbok captain arrives. He is, as they say, "in showroom condition".

"Stay. We've just arrived," he states the bleeding obvious as he points to his minder for the evening.

You politely decline, and decline again.

On another occasion you may be exposed to the torturous assertion of a player's agent that the reason his client killed a police officer was because the man in uniform asked for it.

Mostly, though, El Horno is a splendid drinking hole.

Seating outside is limited, and the cosy inside area is dominated by the long bar counter that runs away from the street, almost the entire length of the inside area towards the kitchen and restrooms at the back. Space is at a premium and if you're standing at the bar you have to take care because those going to and coming from the restrooms can easily cause a spill.

Nobody likes to see that.

Fellow writer Ken Borland and I take up position in a familiar spot. It's busy as the post-dinner revellers start filing in. To our left a group of men in their early twenties, who look like they've been at it since lunch time, are growing increasingly boisterous, some further down the road than others.

One of them is swaying ever so gently. Just when you think he's reached tipping point, he autocorrects the place he physically occupies in the universe. He's looking at us, particularly Borland, in a morbidly curious way. Borland, you see, juts around 1.5 metres (that's a very rough estimate) out of his socks and some folk, especially those who have had a few drinks, can't stop staring.

Eventually the swaying bloke can hold it no more. He heads towards us and as he passes to go to the restrooms he rubs the top of Borland's head. I'm outraged, but temper what's boiling inside.

"I wouldn't do that if I were you," I advise.

It is soon evident the bloke's so drunk he can't speak. Still, he continues to hover with eyes glazed over before turning towards the restrooms. Just as he sets off, though, he lifts his trailing left arm and rubs Borland on the head again before heading off into the human traffic with a bit more purpose. It's the kind of hurried walk of a drunk who knows that if he falls he's likely to fall into someone first.

"He has to come past here. We'll get him on the way back," I assure Borland, who nods enthusiastically in agreement. But we get so caught up in whatever we're discussing that we lose track of the guy's movements. Suddenly, there he is, right next to us.

"You can't just rub people on the head," Borland admonishes.

Speech, however, is an activity beyond the perpetrator. He just sways on the spot. As I am about to berate him again, he turns, heading for his mates a few metres away. Before setting off, this time with his right hand, he rubs Borland on the head again. I'm fuming, but have to remind myself that his mates comfortably outnumber us.

Borland calmly turns to me with the words: "Hold this please, Liam." He hands me his bottle of Monteith's before carefully removing his glasses. (Incidentally, Monteith's are the creators of some very fine beer.)

A familiar ruse is about to be performed but I'm not sure the location – not so much El Horno specifically, but New Zealand in general – is appropriate for Borland's intentions.

With a din around us, Borland beckons the offender closer with his right index finger. For some reason, most people comply when Borland does this, despite the telltale sign he drops. The offender leans in and, as he gets close enough, Borland lunges forward, leading with his considerable cranium-crushing forehead.

At this point I have to stress that head butts are deeply frowned upon in New Zealand. The customary Maori greeting in which noses are pressed together, or "hongi", is at times foolishly mistaken for a head butt. It's not even close. Typically, agent provocateur Boris Johnson, when he was still British foreign secretary, on a visit to New Zealand, once likened the "hongi" to a "Glasgow kiss".

Borland's head butt doesn't disturb the tectonic plates under New Zealand, but it is not for nothing that he is often known by the moniker "Cement Head". In this instance, my first concern isn't for the bloke who staggers backwards frowning, but his mates a few metres away. Thankfully they are all cupping their mouths with laughter, no one showing any interest in helping their mate.

Borland restores his glasses to normal position as he does his Monteith's.

A brief diversion

For the long-distance traveller, losing things and airlines rerouting luggage are par for the course. Few things bring as much angst as waiting at one of the luggage carousels at OR Tambo International. It is a crying shame that the liberation struggle icon's name is now so closely associated with opportunistic plunder, but that's just the way it is.

There are of course other occasions when airlines, or airport baggage handlers, simply drop the ball. Whether you touch down in Vladivostok or Vegas, when your bag doesn't arrive, your heart sinks. That's exactly what happens to four scribes after we touch down in Marseille on an end-of-year tour in 2002. Those who get their bags, myself included, are relieved, but are also filled with dread for what is to come for our travel companions who have their gaze fixed on an empty luggage carousel. At some point, of course, the carousel stops and reality sets in.

We had flown from London Gatwick to France's second city, but still face a 45-minute journey to our hotel. The scribes, who are now travelling unexpectedly light, give their details to the airline's baggage officials as well that of the hotel to which we're heading: the Hotel Dolce Fregate, where the inspiring vistas of the Mediterranean would soon be lost on the men with no back-up underwear.

The Dolce Fregate is a golf estate nestled in the rolling hills overlooking the Med, some 40-odd kilometres east of Marseille. Springbok coach Rudolf Straeuli, on his first

European trip in charge of the team, wants no distractions. This is the build-up to the first match of the tour and he does not want his players wandering the streets of Marseille, or falling for any of the charms of a gritty port city. He presumably also wants to be away from the local press, but being located in the middle of nowhere also means he's going to be stuck with us.

The Dolce Fregate is wonderfully isolated, situated between Saint-Cyr-sur-Mer and the port town of Bandol, the Paul Ricard race circuit in Le Castellet not far to the north. When you leave reception towards the main road, you have to negotiate half a kilometre of limestone road that cuts through vineyards. The region is known for its superb rosés.

At the vehicle entrance, you turn left to Saint-Cyr-sur-Mer or right towards the coast and Bandol. Either way, you face a five-kilometre journey with not much in between apart from the odd bakery. Needless to say taxis can't be hailed in a minute. For men without fresh underwear, who had just travelled around for 15 hours, the portents are grim.

The men are down in the dumps. How could the airline do this? Who's to blame? Did the mix-up occur in Johannesburg or London? Where are the bags now? So many questions …

Whether the bags are on a different continent or in the next town doesn't matter. Their mood remains bleak. The rest of us try in vain to cheer them up with coffee, beer, or the odd croque monsieur. I offer one of them who has a similar body type some of my new underwear bought shortly before the trip. Reassuringly, the tags are still on, but he jokingly declines on the basis that he might not fill them as well as I do. The day after we arrive he takes a taxi to Bandol and then a train to Marseille and buys all but three of the 45 CDs he has on his shopping list.

We neglect to ask whether he buys new underwear.

Goodbye, Tintin

It is time to say goodbye to magnificently manic Mendoza, Argentina. We are all knackered, but are loath to leave. It is a city we feel deeply connected to and it has taken us only a day or so to succumb to its charms. And it has taken that long only because on the Monday of our arrival the locals celebrated San Martin Day in commemoration of the death of one of the country's founding fathers. San Martin, in concert with Simon Bolivár, helped liberate large swathes of South America from Spanish rule and Mendoza was like a ghost town. Those of us in search of local sim cards or adaptors had to wait.

At least we could explore the quiet streets on foot. Because of its location at the foothills of the Andes, the city has no permanent water source; instead it has deep canals that act as arteries from the slopes.

If that helps sustain the city, the sweeping vineyards on its outskirts help feed the soul. It is here that they grow the Malbec varietal, from which they process and bottle a deep, dark-red wine with robust tannins. The grape may have its origins in southwest France, but it is increasingly recognised as an Argentine varietal. A glass of Malbec is best enjoyed with a bife de chorico, a loin steak that melts at the first caress of your tongue. Even visiting South Africans consume the combination as if red wine and meat are new to their palate.

The place has its quirks too. Street dogs roam in large packs and strut around, especially at night, as if they own the place. They are not to be messed with and the locals let them be, almost respectfully so. They make their way from one dustbin to the next, up alleys and back down, on a well coordinated prowl. At intersections they do their magic. They come to a halt and wait for the pedestrian light to turn green before they proceed.

It is not long before we are into the swing of things, so much so that two in our travelling party manage to lose their ATM cards. Unlike the sequence we are used to where the ATM returns your card before it dispenses the cash, here your notes slide out followed by a slip of paper with your balance. Habit then dictates that you put it in your wallet and walk off. That of course causes a day of unnecessary angst but the Argentines aren't overly officious and simple proof of your identity means you can get your card back.

The Argentines are wonderfully hospitable people – until match day, when their English dries up and you are made to feel foreign. They are, after all, out for revenge. In Argentina's first match in the newly formed Rugby Championship in Cape Town the previous week, the Springboks had beaten Los Pumas.

The Argentineans had played well, which gave them hope to turn the tables in Mendoza. Springbok coach Heyneke Meyer is expecting a backlash and much of it around the physicality of the hosts. Keegan Daniel had played No. 8 the previous Saturday, but Meyer thinks more muscle is required for this occasion.

The match itself is a haze of crunching tackles in which the unwieldy Springbok back row of Marcell Coetzee, Jacques Potgieter and Willem Alberts is foiled by the hosts' determined leg tackles. Apart from a lack of variety, the

Springboks' poor handling and lack of composure also conspire against them.

The Boks can hardly penetrate and it is soon apparent that their obsession with trying to bulldoze the opposition is an act in futility. In the end, an intercept try from Frans Steyn, who had played his 50th Test a week earlier, saved Springbok blushes as the match ended 16–all. It is a great effort from the hosts in only their second match in the Rugby Championship.

The six-hour time difference means we have to email our match reports on final whistle, which is always a perilous exercise when the scores are close, or worse, tied, in the closing minutes. The tone of your report will have to be drastically altered if the result swings decisively the other way. Then it's off to the press conference and then the hotel to update copy for Sunday morning's browsers as well as for the Monday papers. This becomes a time-consuming exercise as much of it involves transcribing the press-conference recordings. So sending your last story before you start packing is always a huge relief.

It's late but thankfully the eateries are in sync with the movement of the people. A beer somewhere on Avenida Aristides Villaneuva would top off a wonderful week. We find a bar and then a club where we stay deep into the dark of the morning.

On our way out I'm the first through the door. Outside I pause, in anticipation of the rest to emerge. My attention is, however, diverted to the left by the conversation heading in my direction. It's two Springbok forwards moving with much urgency, which in itself isn't surprising on a morning after a Test match. Rather, it is the tone of the conversation that grabs my attention.

"Kom ons naai hulle," (let's fuck them) one provincial teammate urges the other.

The suggestion is met with a shake of the head and an index finger pointing at his watch. There's nobody accompanying them, which leaves me to believe they have just left a joint where pickings are rich but time in short supply. They disappear down the road, but I think they would do well to make check-out time at the team's Diplomatic Suite Hotel.

Besides, the team's travel arrangements back to South Africa are complicated. It's a flight back to Buenos Aires, then on to São Paulo for a connecting flight to Johannesburg. Curiously, a smaller group, consisting largely of management, is required to make a short hop west over the Andes into Santiago, Chile. From there they will fly to São Paulo and then to Jozi.

My route is a little more conventional, albeit with frustrating stops in Cordoba and Rosario before final touchdown in Buenos Aires where I have planned to spend a few days with my colleague Vata Ngobeni.

Accommodation is only booked at the airport once we reach the capital. We bump into our colleague Craig Lewis, also known as Tintin – a name Vata gives him because of the quiff he suddenly cultivated on tour – who has also somehow found a different way of getting to Buenos Aires.

We all touch down at the Ezeiza International, the city's main airport, and agree to share a minibus into town. It should take us a shade over half an hour all the way on the concrete monstrosity of a motorway that is the Au Luis Dellepiane before it seamlessly becomes Au 25 de Mayo for the last 10 kilometres.

The motorway rises, in parts, high above its surrounds and even buildings four, five storeys high. It offers impressive views of Buenos Aires's flat landscape but also drives home the disparity between the city's haves and have-nots. Not too far away on one side of the motorway you might see tree-lined streets with impressively renovated buildings, while tucked up right against the other side of the motorway poverty looks like it's about to creep up and over. It reminds me a little of home, although their inequality is not quite as stark as South Africa's.

It's dusk, but by the time we are likely to reach Tintin's place of rest the last light would have surrendered to darkness. I'm not familiar with the suburb Tintin will be staying in but given its proximity to Au 25 de Mayo I'm not expecting tree-lined boulevards.

Finally, we take the offramp and immediately it seems we are descending into darkness. This suburb is clearly not as well lit as its neighbours. In the little light there, the urban decay is palpable.

Vata and I look at Tintin to check if he's okay. He grins nervously.

There aren't many folk on the street. It is, after all, Sunday night. On most street corners, however, there'll be a bloke in a vest and shorts who'll step out of a doorway to catch a better view of our vehicle.

Now Vata and I are starting to giggle nervously. Perhaps we are doing it on behalf of Tintin because the driver is slowing down, struggling to read the street numbers. Surely he must be expecting to find our destination any moment now, and it is definitely going to be on this grim, not-so-lit street.

No sooner has he stopped than the driver's out of the

van and opening the back hatch for Tintin's bag. Clearly he doesn't want to stop here longer than he needs to.

Tintin is a little less enthusiastic.

"Are you going to be okay?" one of us enquires.

"Ja, of course," he puts up a brave face.

Of course by now the stationary van has invited the gaze of the few individuals we can pick out in the dark.

Tintin drags his bag to the entrance of the guesthouse. Although the driver is keen to get going, our final enquiry to Tintin about his well being means we hold position. Tintin is standing in front of a massive door, which given its dimension and dark, antique-ish hue, would not be out of place in *Game of Thrones*.

He alerts the establishment of his arrival by tapping a vintage door knocker and they take forever to respond.

Finally the door opens, slightly.

Our van starts rolling forward and Tintin turns to his left to catch a glimpse.

Vata and I both think it, but don't say it as the big doors slam shut. That could be the last time we see Tintin.

Almost banged up in Buenos Aires

When colleague Khanyiso Tshwaku set foot in Argentina on his third work-related international trip, it hadn't dawned on him that the country is rougher than both Mauritius and the United Kingdom, which he had previously visited while on assignment.

He was in the throes of fulfilling a life-long dream of reporting on a match in a far-flung destination for a newspaper he had long admired. In fact, he says, "I almost pissed myself when I got news that I was going to fly to Salta, Argentina for the Springboks' clash against Los Pumas in 2014."

His abiding memory of his journey to Argentina is the expression on the faces of some of the Springbok players not assigned to the match-day squad when they saw the tiny waiting area's straight-back plastic seats at Guarhulhos, São Paulo's International Airport. "After a 10-hour flight from Johannesburg, they had toddler-crying faces when they saw those seats," Tshwaku says.

He too wore a similar face on the Monday after his arrival. "No bacon, no eggs, none of the full English breakfast stuff I'm accustomed to," he lamented, although as a man with a particular devotion to history, he should have known that, apart from soccer, Argentina has little reason to uphold English traditions.

Breakfast apart, his day was soon going to take on a deeper shade of blue. Usually when you arrive at a new destination, connectivity becomes a priority. You need to establish contact with the office, not so much to keep up to date with the latest gossip, but to field requests and transmit your copy.

For some reason, Tshwaku couldn't buy or load data to his phone. And once Tshwaku got connected, his inbox bulged with messages from the office. Not the kind of start you want to make to your tour but, after a long day, tensions eased after he managed to send his copy and it was time for a drink.

He takes up the story: "As we sat at the restaurant enjoying Quilmes [beer], a bloke wearing dark clothes sat at the adjacent table. Jacques van der Westhuyzen [of *The Star*] had a hunch that a crime was about to take place and abruptly cut the conversation.

"'Khanyiso, I think you should watch where you put your

bag,' Van der Westhuyzen warned.

"I blissfully ignored Jacques's warning, even though I kept an eye on the bloke to my left as I continued to quaff the delightful lager."

That was a moment of extreme boldness because the relatively rookie traveller had his passport, foreign exchange and iPad in his laptop bag. He had failed to take it out and place it in his hotel room safe after he checked in.

"Khanyiso, please be careful with that bag. I think the guy across us is up to no good and guys here have creative ways of taking stuff," Van der Westhuyzen sounded another caution.

Tshwaku was using a sling laptop bag with copper-plated holes at the end of the strap. One of those holes, he says, saved his trip.

"The dude pretended to be on his phone and pretended to order something, but somehow I continued to be wilfully ignorant of what was going to happen next. I mean, I grew up in the boxing paradise of Mdantsane and the four times I've been mugged – all at gunpoint – have been within a two-kilometre radius of home. Surely I can't be pickpocketed in some far-off city where people of melanin like me stand out like a trig beacon at the top of a hill," Tshwaku recalls.

"Your bag is going to be taken just about now," Van der Westhuyzen yelled as the bloke walked up and grabbed Tshwaku's bag.

"The slots or holes I mentioned came to my rescue as somehow my middle finger quickly slid in and prevented him from running off with the bag. He yanked once, hurting my finger, but thankfully it didn't budge. The well-dressed bloke quickly disappeared into the teeming evening crowd," Tshwaku remembers.

"You see, I told you! Next time be careful and leave your things at the hotel when you go out," Van der Westhuyzen immediately berated him.

"The Mdantsane stuffing had been knocked out of me, but I still mustered the strength to finish the beer as the near crime became a running joke later on that night," Tshwaku recalls.

Unsung heroes

Two of the unsung heroes in the Springbok setup are Charles Wessels, the senior manager of senior teams, and logistics manager JJ Fredericks, who makes sure all is in order with flights, accommodation, luggage, tackle bags, cones, poles, jerseys, shorts training kit, and the like. It is quite an undertaking. Travel arrangements are made well in advance and are usually executed with military precision.

Fredericks has been in the job since 2008 and knows his way around the rugby-playing world. He insists the job doesn't get easier but that experience helps him trouble shoot potential problems.

Building relationships in his position is absolutely essential. He has an extended list of contacts, from airport and hotel staff to courier companies, airlines and apparel companies, among others, that help smooth the journey for the national team. All the players and the coaches need to worry about is to put in a proper 80-minute performance on match day. The rest is taken care of, running seamlessly behind the scenes, without fuss.

Apart from avoiding hiccups, costs are a major consideration. In the past SA Rugby used to pay a pretty penny for excess luggage but now airline staff are familiar with Fredericks.

The role of the concierge desk can also not be underestimated. In South Africa tips are the usual reward, and it is a service that requires appropriate payment abroad. Around the rugby world, folk at the various concierge desks are on a first-name basis with him and they can be very helpful when things go awry, but there are other things to which Fredericks has to find solutions for himself.

For example, when you are travelling with a tour party of more than 30 people, as the Springboks routinely do, things go missing. When a Springbok squad is announced, Fredericks takes five additional bags containing every size jersey and shorts. He is all too aware of players separating ways with their kit. Often it is just negligence, but players also give items of clothing to friends and relatives.

There are, however, occasions when they are not at fault.

Not having match jerseys or shorts ready before kick-off must be the baggage master's biggest nightmare. In Mendoza in 2012, as is customary, the baggage master arrived at the change room of the Malvinas Stadium to organise warm-up and match apparel. Everything was neatly laid out where the players were to sit before he walked out and locked the door.

He would usually return two hours before the team bus arrived at the ground with the conditioning coach to conclude their preparations. On this occasion, however, as Fredericks and the conditioning coach walked into the change room something was different. Some locals had found a way in and were taking selfies in the Bok change room.

The young men had also helped themselves to some items and, crucially, there were nine match shorts missing. This necessitated a hasty call back to the hotel and one of the additional bags had to be accessed to replenish the lost stock.

Sometimes, however, the unforeseen happens. The team management may, for instance, embark on a course of action oblivious to the impact it might have further down the line.

The Springboks took a Rhino scrum machine to Australia. The Aussies have never been keen on scrumming – they generally view it as a means to restart play – and a similar machine of the same brand wasn't available so the Springbok management had one sent over in advance.

What they didn't factor in, though, was the cost of having the machine returned to South Africa. The courier costs and customs duty added up to a prohibitive amount.

The machine is rusting away in Australia.

Two

Planes, Trains and Automobiles

The process of getting to your destination is often as much part of the trip as the time spent there. On rugby tours we mostly find ourselves on planes, taxis and the occasional train and, for very different reasons, you have to keep your wits about you.

Cleared for take-off

EVEN IF IT WAS just temporarily, we were a little sad to leave Buenos Aires. Duty called. After a hectic few days and nights in the Argentine capital, it was off to Tucumán, where the Springbok midweek team was to face Argentina A.

Although the midweek team on the end-of-year tour in 2000 spent limited time with the Test team, head coach Harry Viljoen stressed the importance of a good start to the epic five-week odyssey. It would be good for morale and confidence would permeate the camp, he figured.

We were to fly out from Jorge Newbery Airport, which is used for domestic as well as regional departures to Uruguay, just a short hop over the River Plate. A year earlier, though, a Boeing 737 operated by Líneas Aéreas Prividas on its take-off roll failed to get airborne. It smashed through the airport's perimeter fencing and hit a car as it crossed a freeway before finally coming to rest against road-construction vehicles. The pilots had failed to set the flaps to its take-off configuration and, as much as they pulled back on the controls, the plane was pretty much doomed by their earlier negligence. Their inaction resulted in 65 deaths.

A day or two before we were to depart for Tucumán, I cheerily shared the story with colleague Gavin Rich who was, and I suspect still is, petrified of flying. He was unimpressed and vowed to make the necessary pharmaceutical interventions before the flight. He told us that Springbok World Cup-winning wing James Small also had a fear of flying and that they had once shared stories about their phobia on a flight while gripping tightly to the arm rests.

Gavin had popped his pills by the time we arrived at Jorge Newbery. He was ready for this, whether the men in the cockpit were going to deploy the flaps or not. The only mild concern he had was whether his medication would kick in in time for the one-hour-50-minute flight. His concern was a little misplaced. The flight, as the information display inside the terminal informed us, was delayed by more than an hour. This now meant he had to stay awake until we boarded.

I decided to stick by him through this ordeal. I had to keep him moving, but Jorge Newbery, although a perfectly functional regional airport with picturesque views of the River Plate, wasn't designed for passengers who need to while away time. Our walk to keep the already-groggy Gav on his feet wasn't very far because it wasn't long before we reached the end of the terminal.

I – a little mischievously, I admit – tried to cheer him up by pointing out a single-prop Cessna parked no more than 50 metres away, and suggested that if they can't fix our plane some of us may have to go on the four-seater. I know he was unimpressed because the medication had by now limited his vocal range to groans.

Finally, we got the all clear. We were allowed to board the Aerolineas Argentinas Boeing 737 from the front or the rear. As I made my way up the rear stairway, I shared the story of the crash the previous year with Springbok utility back Deon Kayser. He too was unimpressed – I know because of his silence and the way he frowned.

I was sitting at the back of the aircraft, and could see Gavin in one of the window seats five or so rows up. His head was already resting against the window. Thankfully, he was sleeping and didn't have to go through the ordeal of taking off because we had been assigned to Runway 13 and were taking off in the same direction the crash had taken place the previous year.

We turned left onto Runway 13 and there we stopped for what seemed an eternity. Everything seemed fine – the cabin crew was strapped in, the engines were rotating at a low rev as they were supposed to – but there seemed to be a delay the folk in the cockpit were not sharing.

The wait dragged on and it was getting uncomfortably hot in the plane. If we were going to be here much longer, we needed to either return to a parking bay or open some of the doors.

Finally, however, an announcement in Spanish. The engines spooled up purposefully and the 737 slowly got off the mark. As it built up speed, though, its age became even more apparent. My proximity to the galley left me exposed to the din from the catering paraphernalia shaking violently behind vaguely hinged doors that created the impression that they were about to pop.

Naturally, the increase in speed made for higher decibels from the back.

By now, too, the take-off roll seemed longer than usual. I figured, however, that the presence of 25 burly men as well as bags filled with weighty equipment meant we had to eat up more tarmac before we could get safely airborne. I, though, had an aisle seat and couldn't see the wings to determine whether our flaps had been deployed to the required five-degree angle.

What I could vaguely see to the left was the always murky River Plate. It was just a blur and I figured that we by now must have gone through V1, that critical moment when the plane reaches a speed at which it is no longer safe to abort take-off. It was now on to V2, the threshold speed at which it is safe for the pilots to pull the controls back and get the plane airborne.

Just as my thoughts turned to how Isabel Perón was deposed as president in a coup at this very site, I sensed the nose of the plane pitching up. Still the main wheels languished on terra firma, but seconds later and to great relief to all on board the wheels tucked into the underbelly of the plane. By then the only audible sound apart from the rattle from the galley was Gavin snoring.

Touch-and-go Kai Tak

The opportunity to fly to Hong Kong left me with the dual thrill of flying to an airport where it is notoriously tricky to land and experiencing a night life that only relents when the sun is on the rise.

This was my first work assignment out of the country and Hong Kong beckoned because of the World Sevens Series leg to be held there. Local newspapers wouldn't ordinarily dispatch reporters to events for which they cared little – the Sevens scene back then simply did not have the following or indeed investment it has today – but title sponsors Cathay Pacific were happy to have us there.

Occasionally, for big tournaments, the Springbok Sevens team would be loaded with heavyweights known for their heroics in the 15-man game, but generally Sevens was the domain of lither men. Coach Dawie Snyman had to make do with what was tossed his way, but in Dion O'Cuinneagain he had a genial captain who was widely respected. O'Cuinneagain's rugby prowess as player and captain would later see him lead Ireland at the 1999 RWC.

Despite having tea spilt over my legs by a horrified and deeply apologetic flight attendant, I was excited to catch a glimpse of the Hong Kong rooftops as we made final approach into the now defunct Kai Tak Airport, named incidentally after Messrs Kai and Tak. We had been warned, however, to expect showers on arrival in Hong Kong, so the prospect of seeing the skyscraper rooftops, so often featured in movies, travel shows and advertisements, looked increasingly bleak. Besides, I had a middle-section aisle seat, and the low-hanging cloud further complicated matters. I would not be able to see into apartment dwellers' kitchens or watch them watch television as was often the case for window-seat passengers on inbound flights to Kai Tak.

Resigned to this visual impairment, I closed my eyes and dropped my neck back before we touched down. The Boeing 747 was being buffeted, but because this was my first international flight I thought it normal. The plane was, however, tipping its wings disconcertingly, so it came as some relief to hear the engines spool down in anticipation of rubber meeting tarmac.

But there was no thud; instead, my stomach experienced the same sensation you get when a roller coaster bottoms out. One moment we were going to touch down and the next the engines had sprung back to life and, amid quite a few "oohs" and "aahs", the plane's nose was pointing skyward again.

Must be an aborted landing, I thought. Wow! Never mind looking into nearby apartments, this is the business.

If we had just aborted our landing it would be for sound reasons. Kai Tak airport's single runway was precariously placed, with mountains and skyscrapers to the north and the runway jutting out into Victoria Harbour in Kowloon.

The proximity of the mountains precluded a direct approach from the north, which meant that pilots had to come in from the west and line the aircraft up with a huge checkerboard on the side of a hill. With the plane just 3.5 kilometres away from the threshold of the runway, pilots have to perform a low-altitude precision 47-degree right turn.

Three years earlier a Chinese Airlines pilot got it horribly wrong and overshot the runway instead of going around, while eight years earlier another aircraft collided with runway lights and slid into the sea, claiming seven lives.

We climbed for about a minute-and-a-half before the captain took to the PA system. It has always astonished me that aircraft are built at such great expense and then, as an afterthought, they throw in the cheapest PA system. It makes for much muffled sound and only every third word is audible.

I think this is what the captain said: "Ladies and gentlemen, you would have noticed we are no longer landing. We've had to abort the landing because I did not deem it safe. It is monsoon season here and this weather is not uncommon.

"You are probably wondering about our fuel after more than 14 hours of flying. Well, it's a little low. But don't worry, we will fly to Guangzhou, which isn't too far away, on the mainland.

"There we'll put in enough fuel to get us back to Hong Kong. Sorry for the inconvenience."

Getting bumped

The Heathrow Express is rolling west. I'm happy to be onboard. The service has been in operation for just over a year, but to me it feels like launch day.

I'm set to board a British Midland flight to Dublin where Ireland is meeting Australia in a RWC clash later in the afternoon. Two colleagues are reporting on the Springboks in Scotland, so I have licence for this diversion.

The check-in queue is dispiritingly long though. The process is slow and increasingly passengers at the front are having animated conversations with a sheepish-looking bloke inside a reflector jacket. Just my luck. He's sharing bleak news: the flight has been overbooked and we'll have to go on standby.

I look around to see how many others are on board HMS

Unnecessary Anguish. There are about 15 of us, which means it is unlikely all of us will make it on board. I nudge towards the front to try to hear what the flight controller is saying. He's talking to two stocky women who look as though they're in their twenties. They are also on their way to the rugby. Their Wallaby jerseys suggest as much.

When I do manage to have a word I explain that I need to get to Lansdowne Road, and that this is work, that my job may be on the line, unlike the two fans to my left. But my story doesn't seem to fully capture the flight controller's full attention, let alone imagination. I know I'm in trouble when he keeps nodding but looking elsewhere.

Of course, once they determine how many of us can board the two Sheilas jump like *Amazing Race* winners when they are handed their boarding passes. I miss out in this lottery – I am now definitely going to miss kick-off. I have my big suitcase with me so I ask, if it is not too much of an imposition, British Midland to arrange a taxi for when I arrive in Dublin. That would save valuable time and the flight controller in his reflector jacket nods again.

Of course, once I retrieve my bag on the other side, and head to the carrier's counter to enquire about my taxi, I'm met by a shrug of the shoulders and a shake of the head. So I join the queue and figure I'd be lucky to see any of the first half at Lansdowne Road.

Finally, a chatty, grey-haired gentleman slides my bag into his boot. I explain my predicament. "Sure, that's no problem. I'll drop you at Lansdowne Road, and then I'll take your bag to the Burlington."

He explains that it is a little over a mile from the stadium to the hotel and that it shouldn't take long after I disembark for the bag to be delivered. I nod, but my unease isn't so much the distance as the fact that I will be leaving my bag in the care of a complete stranger.

I get out at Lansdowne Road, pay for my trip as well as the onward journey of my bag. I also leave a generous tip before I head for the turnstiles.

Of course, I get any number of curious looks as I head up the rickety wooden steps in search of my seat in the Main Stand. I know the Lansdowne Road Stadium is old but this feels like kindle in the making.

I have barely sat down when Welsh referee Clayton Thomas brings the first half to a close. Amazingly, I have only missed two penalties, one from Matt Burke and, I presume, a long-range one from John Eales.

Second-half tries by Tim Horan and Ben Tune help seal the deal in a 23–3 win that sees the Wallabies top their pool and secure their place in the quarterfinals.

"If we are going to be there at the end we still have a lot of improving to do," Australia coach Rod Macqueen notes presciently in the press conference. Improve they did.

Ireland, however, are now in for an uncomfortable wait. "For us to go through we'll have to do it the hard way," says the then Ireland coach Warren Gatland.

With the press conference done and my copy filed, I head for the Burlington, albeit with a little trepidation. Did my cabby do what he was so generously tipped to do?

As I walk up to the entrance the Burlington's doorman springs into action from the inside. A strapping fella dressed in black under a top hat holds the door with the welcome: "Mr Del Carme, we've been expecting you."

To this day I don't know how he knew.

Finding our Chacras

Travelling to and watching Springbok practices can be a chore. That is because we are usually only tolerated early in the week when the combatants from the previous weekend are still in recovery mode and we are often limited to only the first 20 minutes of practice when the players warm up.

With nothing to glean from the warm-ups you are often left wondering whether the effort and the money spent to get there were worth it. But if you do pick up something that has escaped your colleagues' attention at practice, it can feel like a gold nugget in your pocket.

You do, however, run the risk of being shown the gate after 20 minutes. On some days coaches are more than happy to have the media at training sessions but on others, particularly when they are under pressure, they wish you were on a different continent. Photographers and cameramen in particular run the risk of being pointed to the exit when the warm-up is completed. Only SuperSport, who by virtue of being the official broadcast-rights holders, enjoy near unfettered access.

Writers, on the other hand, are exposed to the whims of the coach. When the coach is on the back foot, writers can expect a short stay. On the occasions we are asked to leave, we know the coach is likely to have a trick up his sleeve. That usually takes the shape of a left-field selection, rather than some outlandishly intricate move aimed at bamboozling the opposition.

On one occasion, in August 2012, we are keen to see how coach Heyneke Meyer will set out his stall for the return match against Argentina in Mendoza. It is a sunny Tuesday afternoon when we set off to the Chacras Rugby Club on the outskirts of Mendoza. Unless you rent a car, the only way to get there is by taxi.

Our driver is on time but we urge him to get a move on. He's way too caught up in the moment of having visitors from the southern tip of Africa in his vehicle. He talks non-stop, in Spanish, and we need to get to the club before the Boks' warm-up finishes. The Boks had beaten Argentina in Cape Town the previous weekend but the hosts had been a little unconvincing and changes are inevitable.

This is to be Meyer's first away Test in charge of the Springboks and naturally he is keen to get things right. He is expecting Los Pumas to come hard at his team. "I want to get the players more mentally tough. I mean no disrespect to the previous coaches but we need to toughen up," says Meyer.

Meyer's plea for a stronger physical presence from his team is in part also due to the fact that they will be without the battleship qualities of Bismarck du Plessis who got injured the previous Saturday at Newlands.

It now falls to players like loose forward Willem Alberts to step forward and occupy the Bok front line. Earlier in the day Alberts had raised an eyebrow at the criticism levelled at the Boks in the wake of their 27–6 triumph over Los Pumas in Cape Town the previous Saturday. The scoreline seemed convincing enough but some pundits felt the Boks weren't slick enough against opponents in their first ever match in the Rugby Championship.

"There will always be criticism but we can take it on the chin. We can now just build and go forward," says Alberts.

At practice we are particularly keen to see what back-row formation will be put through its paces and our suspicions are confirmed two days later when Meyer opts for the wrecking-ball qualities of Alberts at No. 8, a position he occupied with distinction when he started his provincial career with the Lions. Two more back-row battering rams in Jacques Potgieter and Marcell Coetzee are earmarked for the Test.

We agree a pick-up time with the same taxi driver and, satisfied that we have seen enough, head for the exit on the sprawling grounds of the Chacras club. Then, as we near the agreed pick-up point, we notice a group of middle-aged men sitting in a circle. They are deep in discussion and their conversation has been greased by a bottle of Fernet-Branca, the bitter herbal liqueur, often softened by Coke in those parts, being passed around in its neatest form.

Their attention shifts to us and they look intrigued. They ask whether we are from the land of the Springboks and we confirm, "Si."

"Ah," says the fella now in possession of the bottle as he waves us closer.

The folk in Mendoza are extremely hospitable and anyone vaguely associated with the Springbok badge are just about handed the keys to the city. In fact, even Mendoza's four-legged creatures take a shine to the Springboks. On one bus ride to training at the Chacras Club a dog decided to run all the way in front of the vehicle.

Obviously we're a little reluctant to join the men getting day-drunk. A SuperSport commentator has warned us of the stomach-turning properties of Fernet-Branca and even from a distance it smells like Borstol-meets-Absinthe-meets-Jeyes Fluid. Also, our taxi is due to arrive soon and we have copy to file.

The señor with the bottle doesn't look like he's going to take "no" for an answer though. Besides, his impressive moustache and Stetson bestow on him the look of a ranchero who'd adroitly swing his rope and drag us in if he had to. It is clear he wants us to have a shot of Fernet. As a compromise, we nudge closer, careful not to display overt signs of enthusiasm by sitting.

As we soon discover, the taste of Fernet induces an immediate change in facial expression. You are left with an involuntary grimace when it hits your tongue. "Tiger smile!" says the man under the Stetson as the first journo reveals his teeth.

Beside the pourer, the bloke next in line for a swig bristles into action. He's lamenting the fact that these foreigners are partaking of the delicious tipple for which he has now been overlooked. The pourer firmly brushes him aside and now the others too are ganging up on him.

We all gulp down a shot, and say, "Gracias," before nudging to our pick-up point.

Our chatty driver arrives, and it seems he's been at the Fernet too. He is even more animated and talkative than he was when he dropped us off. He'll say something in Spanish, point to a landmark he deems important and laugh with a spine-tingling screech. This, of course, sets us off too.

We don't understand a word he's saying but he continues to point randomly at a building or statue for which he thinks we require an explanation. Occasionally, he'll take his hands off the steering wheel, gesticulating as if that will provide a fool-proof translation.

When we reach the city he suddenly has more things to point at. Problem is, he's still driving at the same manic speed and now resorts to dipping in and out of lanes, still nattering away.

His screeching stops only when he slams the brakes in front of one of our hotels. We get out chuckling. Little do we know that our next experience of a taxi driver in Mendoza will be almost the opposite.

It's match day and we've booked our ride in advance. We wait in vain and have to take to the streets to hail a taxi. When we finally get a bloke to stop he complains about having to sit in traffic en route to the game.

Estadio Malvinas Argentinas is located inside the impressive San Martin Park, the stadium specifically built for the 1978 Soccer World Cup and named to reflect Argentina's claims of sovereignty over the Falkland Islands, which gets me wondering whether England has ever been invited to play there.

After witnessing a bizarre match in which fortunes fluctuate before ending in stalemate and the press conference done, our attention shifts to the next potential problem – getting a taxi back to town. Even the locals tell us it is going to involve an inordinate amount of luck, but we need to get back to our hotel rooms to send follow-up stories that will await copy editors the next morning. Given the time difference, it is best done now.

One of us casually asks a member of the Springbok support staff if we can catch a ride with them so, in amongst the tackle bags, padding, flexi and marker cones, slalom poles and bibs, we head back, crisis thankfully averted.

Waiting in rain

It became the trend in the latter part of the twentieth century for new stadiums to be constructed in the middle of nowhere

– often on industrial wasteland, where land is cheap and bulldozers do what they do without conscience.

Two prime examples, in a rugby sense, are Stade de France and Stadium Australia.

When it comes to Stade de France, if your accommodation is anywhere near the centre of Paris, you are in for at least a half-hour train ride with a change-over at Gare du Nord. The last time I made my way there from central Paris, I travelled by car, and somehow my friend Damien Dussault found a conveniently located McDonald's where he left his car for the duration of the match.

Tests scheduled for November in Paris kick off late. They get underway at 9pm, which potentially of course gives you time to explore the city, but it also means you have to walk the deadline tightrope late in the evening. In fact, most Sunday editions back home are unlikely to carry match reports on games that kick off 10pm SA time.

Of course once the game is done you have to wait for the coaches and captains to have their say in the press conferences, followed by what is called a mixed zone in which players – often en route to the team bus – are supposed to stop and chat in a more relaxed environment. This too can be time consuming, which means your prospects of making the last train back to Gare du Nord are fairly remote.

Stade de France, which incidentally until 2019 was the only stadium to have hosted a football and a RWC final (Yokohama Stadium became the second), is located in Saint-Denis to the north of Paris, so you don't have to venture too far from the stadium to be confronted with northern Paris's urban decay.

On my last visit three South African media stragglers

were hoping to make it back to Billancourt, southwest of the centre of Paris. We knew that catching a train was no longer an option so that meant hailing a taxi or Uber driver. Now, taxi drivers generally don't drive around Stade de France after midnight, but finally one of my colleagues managed to get his app to play ball. There was one Uber driver in the vicinity, but locating each other was proving problematic.

Eventually, though, another responded to our need. Most of our journey back to Billancourt was on a motorway and we all got out at the hotel of the bloke who had arranged the ride. By this time the rain that had earlier been no more than mist carried a heavier payload. I had a quarter-hour walk to my hotel and I couldn't help think of the same predicament I had found myself in during the 1999 RWC.

The Boks had beaten England in the quarterfinal – thanks largely to Jannie de Beer's five drop goals – and there was much to write in the immediate aftermath.

It was deep into the night. Colleague Barney Spender and I made our way to Stade de France station in the hope of still getting back into town by rail. As we stood on an empty platform, watched by a gang of delinquents on the adjacent platform, the Springboks' win seemed a distant memory.

Barney knew the lay of the land but we were on this platform more in hope than conviction. It started raining and, although we were under cover, we knew that we would need to move at some point – heaven knew what we were in for if the delinquents decided to cross platforms.

The problem was that our hotel was almost eight kilometres away, near the splendid La Madeleine, and it was unlikely we were going to encounter a taxi near the stadium at that hour. Tackling the distance on foot would probably be the softest bullet we would have to bite, so we set off. We tried to cheer each other up with light, inconsequential conversation but it wasn't long before we were both wet and glum.

We walked, head down, feet squelching, hoping our laptops were still dry. This was not what I had in mind on my first visit to Paris, and I was falling out of love with the City of Love. It continued to rain, but eventually the urban landscape began to change. Suddenly there were street lamps and then music. An oasis.

Because we were still proceeding heads down we passed the entrance of the brassiere where the music was coming from. Just as we realised we had walked right past the door we both stopped dead in our tracks. We glanced at each other and a nod confirmed that we should turn and enter.

There was a band playing and although the chanson was a little folksy, it was sufficiently upbeat for involuntary tapping of feet and bobbing of heads. Thankfully one side of the bar counter was near the entrance. The lights were dimmed, but it was from the small stage that this place generated its glow.

This was a bit of Paris that had escaped us earlier in the week. For all we knew, Johnny Hallyday could be next on. For now, though, a man grey on the edges, but holding on to a swagger that would have served him well in the 1970s, was holding the microphone and swaying. To our right, on the other hand, was a young man still trying to escape boyhood. His right foot tapped perfectly to the rhythm and it would have been odd if it hadn't. With his left hand, he was keeping upright a case containing his double bass.

He looked nervous, yet excited, waiting to get the nod. Song after song, however, he'd been made to wait. Now it was just getting awkward. Finally, and mercifully, he was called on to generous applause, as much for the old-timer as for the youngster.

He hurriedly removed his instrument from its case and stepped up without missing a beat. Somewhere out there, in a different arrondissement of this enchanting city, the Boks and possibly some of our colleagues were partying their socks off.

Barney and I, however, wouldn't be anywhere else.

Marooned in Manly

In Sydney, Stadium Australia – or ANZ Stadium, as it is called during the 2003 World Cup – is a 50-minute train ride from Central Station. I undertook that journey once and before long grew concerned that I may not be on the right train. Only when the train made its way through the area of Homebush was I comfortable I was on the right track.

Of course that journey and the ensuing walk to the ticket office took so long that I was met by a sign at the kiosk that told me I had missed closing time by five minutes. Ah well. Back home through Homebush.

Some in the South African media corps were so desperate to stay in the Springbok team hotel in Sydney during this RWC that they clearly didn't think through their travel arrangements to and from the stadium.

The team had set up camp in eastern Sydney overlooking the ocean in Manly's Pan Pacific Hotel. While the team could simply board their coach and drive for around an hour to the stadium, the hacks had the option of getting on a bus (if they were prepared to spend the time) or a taxi (if they were prepared to spend the money) and travel to Central Station from where they would have to catch a train to the stadium.

The other option, which was the more prudent, was to walk 10-or-so minutes to the ferry terminal and then make their way across the bay on a 20-minute ride to Circular Quay. From there they would have to catch a train to Central Station for a connecting service to the stadium.

For the rest of us who stayed in town, getting to the stadium was a far more straightforward affair, but the problem facing the blokes who chose to stay in Manly was that they would run the risk of missing the last ferry departing Circular Quay. Even when the Boks played a pool match against Georgia at the more conveniently situated Sydney Football Stadium (then the Aussie Stadium), the men from Manly started complaining about their potential fate in the knockout stages.

The match against Georgia was Schalk Burger's debut Test and he went on to represent the Springboks another 85 times, mostly with thunderous distinction. The occasion also marked the first time John Smit donned the captain's armband from the start and he was to do so on 82 more occasions.

We had to make our way from Sydney to a pool match in Brisbane where Samoa's Brian Lima almost tackled Derick Hougaard into the nearest infirmary and then on to Melbourne where Carlos Spencer, in throwing the ball between his legs, helped usher the Boks to the tournament exit.

With the Boks knocked out, the men from Manly didn't have to worry about catching the last ferry. Neither did they bother to attend the semifinals or final of the RWC as a result, and when one of us enquired whether they were going to attend the third-place play-off between New Zealand and France we were met with a firm, "Nee, fok dit!" (No, fuck that!)

Percy and the badger

It's the day after the Boks beat Fiji in a RWC pool match in Wellington in 2011. They comfortably win 49–3 but not before the islanders fly into tackles with seeming homicidal intent. The Boks, however, keep their composure and their campaign is well and truly underway, and so are we.

We have to drive the 640-odd kilometres from Wellington to Auckland, the two biggest cities on North Island. In four days the Boks are due to play Namibia in North Harbour and they will be setting up camp in Auckland.

We've been told that our trip should take around six to seven hours if we stay on State Highway 1, and we're looking forward to the road trip. This is probably the best part of covering a World Cup – the opportunity to see the country for what it is away from the major centres. Besides, there is the breathtaking beauty to take in too: North Island is littered with volcanoes, cliffs, pointy peninsulas and vast lakes.

We head north through the Ngauranga interchange and then its eponymous gorge towards Johnsonville. Soon we reach Paekakariki, a small town with under 2 000 inhabitants but partly placed on the map because it is where try-scoring machine Christian Cullen learnt how to run circles around – and then away from – would-be tacklers. If you blink, you'll miss Paekakariki.

The road then bends inland and we cross the Otaki and Manawatu rivers as we head for a place of horrendous puns called Bulls. When you are greeted by a sign that reads "A town like no udder" and one like "Const-A-Bull" outside the police station, then "Reliev-A-Bull" outside a public toilet is not out of place. I could swear there was a convenience store called "Whatta load of Bull".

Somewhere in Bulls we hit a right as the motorway resumes and for quite a stretch we have the Rangitikei River as a calming companion to our right. At some point on our journey, and I cannot be sure exactly where, we almost end up in a river.

If that sounds a little dramatic, bear with me. I'm sitting at the back, with fellow *Sunday Times* hack Louis de Villiers to my right. We're going through the Sunday papers, driving through rural nothingness, when De Villiers exclaims, "WHAT?"

He then snorts, and starts laughing uncontrollably. Naturally, I enquire what's tickling his funny bone.

"Christ on a bike!" he says. "You're never gonna believe this." And delivers another rapid burst of laughter.

He then reads: "The dwarf porn-star doppelgänger of Gordon Ramsay has reportedly been found dead in a badger's den in Wales."

Almost immediately the other occupants of the car start giggling. De Villiers continues: "Percy Foster, 35, who is a dead-ringer for the UK celebrity chef, was found by Ministry of Agriculture staff ahead of a planned badger-eradication programme near Tregaron, West Wales, British tabloid *Sunday Sport* reported.

"According to the paper, Mr Foster was clothed but had been 'partially gnawed' by animals."

Now the car is consumed by a cacophony of laughter. De

Villiers composes himself before continuing: "Adult movie producer Dexter Yamunkeh told *Sunday Sport* the actor was a 'little guy with big problems'."

The laughter intensifies.

De Villiers, though, soldiers on: "'He was doing well but he was under pressure, 24/7, like everyone in this goddamned business.'"

By then tears are rolling down my cheeks and I suspect the driver has also surrendered to the hilarity because he suddenly yanks the steering wheel to the right. We're on a slight decline and narrowly miss the white pillar that marks the start of a small bridge.

Thankfully, there is no traffic going the other way and we have barely crossed the small bridge when our laughter continues.

Later that week it is revealed the Percy Foster story is a complete hoax. We almost died driving off a bridge for nothing.

The worst ever

I can wait another 10 or 15 minutes, perhaps even half an hour, but it's unlikely the rain will stop anytime soon. This, after all, is Cardiff and it's November. What else do you expect? Besides, the place I'm in is about to close.

We've had a splendid evening. A few journalists, a couple of members of the Springbok management team and some locals. The place, however, is about to close and if I were to walk back to my apartment on the other side of the Principality Stadium and the river Taff, it will probably take me close to 20 minutes.

Ordinarily, it is a distance I'm happy to walk, but in this

rain that would not be an option. Thankfully there are taxis close by.

I'm beaten to the first one by a couple who needs to get somewhere quickly. The next one pulls up and I explain to the driver that I'm staying on a lane on the other side of the stadium, but that he couldn't access it from next to the river on Duke Street; he needs to do it further down. That means he will have to drive slightly past before turning back.

We're off, but almost immediately I'm alarmed that the driver who I thought was either Pakistani or Bangladeshi heads in the opposite direction. That is a feeling I often get in taxis because I'm generally well wired when it comes to locating my magnetic north.

Initially, I don't say anything but I'm growing increasingly alarmed that he's not turning towards Cardiff Castle or the CBD. Soon we are in a residential area that I don't recognise. After one or two turns, still nothing looks familiar. I say something along the lines: "Are you sure this is the best route?"

The driver turns his head left but not all the way around. He's heard me but he's not responding. Less than a minute later I ask again, but this time more to the point: "Are we going the right way?"

He mumbles something and I ask again. He stops abruptly. As he gets out I think I hear him say, "Get out." When he opens my door, it is clear that is what he said. "I'm not taking you any further."

"Are you for real?" I ask. "You're dropping me off in the middle of nowhere?"

I neglect to add "in the rain" but that's going to make no difference in this situation. The guy is pissed off and our ways are about to separate.

At this point we are talking over each other and before long we're shouting. As he retreats to his minivan I tell him he's the world's worst taxi driver. (I figure this is fair on the basis of driving the passenger further away from the intended destination, having the gall to get pissed off when questioned about it and then throwing out the passenger now in driving rain.)

He speeds off and I try to take a picture of his number plate but the rain puts paid to that idea. It's all a blur, as has been the last five minutes.

I have to pinch myself that this has actually happened. I'm in a suburb I have not been to before in the middle of the night. Although a foreigner, I know the Cardiff CBD and surrounding areas reasonably well, having travelled there for the first time in 1996 on a cricket tour and several subsequent rugby tours. Besides, it is now almost impossible to get lost because since 1999 the stadium's four 90-metre masts, as well as 3.2 kilometres of tension cables in each corner, are visible from miles away.

The problem is I'm almost surrounded by double-storey dwellings. I can't be sure but I think I'm to the west of the CBD so I start retracing my steps to where I think that idiot of a taxi driver picked me up. After the first couple of turns, still nothing looks familiar.

The rain is now bucketing down, but thankfully I'm wearing a proper rain jacket. From covering many rugby tours in cold climes, I have bought jackets fitting every continent. The Kathmandu one I'm wearing I purchased in New Zealand and while the rain can't penetrate the jacket, the water is flowing generously onto my jeans and down into my shoes. Although I've deployed the jacket's hoodie and the rain is pelting down on my head I can still hear the squelching of my feet in my shoes.

I've been going for about 10 minutes and grow concerned that I'm heading in the wrong direction. In the distance I see someone crossing the street. Damn, an opportunity lost to ask a local. I press on in the direction I think I ought to go.

Now I've been at it for almost half an hour and I'm approaching an intersection. I'm not sure if I should go straight or turn right. Definitely not left.

At the intersection I look to my right and there's a bloke heading my way. Thank goodness. But can he help? I ask him the way to the Millennium Stadium (I figured the locals still call it by its old name). He turns to his left and points up. There it is. Those giant masts that lend the structure the look of a gigantic sailboat.

When you walk in the rain you tend to walk with your head down and had I looked up I might have spotted it sooner. Still, I'm hugely relieved and thank the stranger.

Now I need to establish what corner of the stadium I'm looking at and it takes another quarter of an hour before I get out of my wet jeans. As I climb into the warm shower I wonder where I might have been had I shut up and allowed that taxi driver to go on his merry way.

Generally speaking

The Boks are back in Argentina and are off to Salta in the country's northwest.

It is a difficult destination to get to for South Africans. In the past, South African Airways, before they became wholly reliant on bailouts, operated the route between Johannesburg and Buenos Aires. But that is long gone and the stricken airline has opted to use São Paulo as a hub for South Africans who want to travel to South America. If you live in Cape Town or Durban you'll have to board four flights to get to Salta.

An executive whose company's name is emblazoned on the Springboks' apparel opted to make the journey to the far-flung destination where the Boks have played in 2014, 2016, 2017 and 2019. After having got on and off so many planes, he was probably unaware of the fine print on his last boarding pass. He was travelling from Buenos Aires to Salta, but lost track of the fact that the plane was to touch down in Tucumán first.

Once the plane came to a halt after an hour and 40 minutes and the seat-belt signs had been switched off, he reached for his carry-on luggage. No doubt announcements were being made in Spanish through the aircraft's public address system about folk travelling to Salta needing to stay on board.

The executive, by now weary from all the travelling, headed for the exit, said his goodbyes at the door and made his way down the steps to the tarmac. At this point it should really have occurred to him to look up to the top of the building where there should ordinarily be a clue to the location of the strip of tarmac you have just landed on.

Argentina has a particular devotion to their generals and in this instance Teniente General Benjamín Matienzo International would not have helped him much, unless of course he was into that sort of thing. Had he known his army generals, it would have dawned on him that he wasn't about to enter the arrivals hall at Salta's Martín Miguel de Güemes International.

His blunder was about to make things worse.

He headed for the taxi rank. There he shared the name and address of the hotel at which he had a reservation and they headed off.

When the driver turned right to head north the executive might have realised something was amiss. If he wasn't alarmed then, then surely once the taxi bisected the suburbs of San José to the west and Las Talitas to the east he must have realised the folly of his ways. It can be reasonably assumed that a question like, "Is the hotel a little outside town?" would have emerged from the back seat.

I reckon once there were no buildings in sight, with Lake El Cadillal in the east, the executive must have resigned himself to the fact that he was in for the long haul. It's not like there is a flight every hour to Salta.

At least three flights and a leisurely 320-kilometre, three-hour-45-minute taxi ride later he arrived at his hotel.

Three
"No, You Didn't!"

It never ceases to astound me how normal, rational, clear-thinking people can be so prone to folly when they are on the other side of the world. You'd swear there is something in the water.

The Knight of Northbridge

PERTH HOLDS FEW DELIGHTS. And if you find some, the local constabulary will soon snuff out any prospect of joy.

It was once described by a fellow writer as "Bloemfontein with a river". Greater Perth boasts a shade over two million inhabitants. Indigenous Australians have inhabited the area for more than 30 000 years, but it wasn't until 2006 that the Federal Court of Australia brought down a judgment recognising Noongar native title over the Perth metropolitan area.

The estuary of the majestic Swan River carves a graceful path through the eastern fringes of the CBD en route to its mouth in Fremantle. The river, which got its name from the black swans in the area, provides residents with all manner of recreational activity, whether you're a cyclist or a runner.

But we're not in town for that. The Wallabies are due to clash with the Springboks, but the match is struggling to embed itself in the consciousness of West Australians. This, too, is footy country, with the Fremantle Dockers the biggest ticket in town. Reserve hooker Saia Fainga'a walked into a hotel elevator in 2013 wearing his Wallaby tracksuit when a local asked him, "Mate, who do you play for?"

As ever, I only have a handful of writing colleagues on this tour. One of them is Jason Humphries. He doesn't tour often with the Boks and is stoked to be along.

Humphries is a wonderfully gregarious fella, a man who holds firm opinions, often hardened further by schooners of Tooheys beers. He is a demonstrative talker, generally using his hands to help illustrate a point. Often it looks like he is blessing a mass audience.

One night while staring into his beer Humphries lets it be known that he has to leave soon. He seems concerned about hailing a taxi prepared to take him to his guesthouse in the suburbs. We don't share his concern and tell him as much. Still he's uneasy about persuading a driver to take him some distance away from all the bars and restaurants in buzzing Northbridge. Eventually, though, we say our goodbyes and the rest of us head for the bridge that will take us back into the city.

Humphries arrives at the next day's press conference looking a little bedraggled. We drag the reason for his disorderly and sheepish state out of him.

He owns up.

When his taxi had dropped him off at his guesthouse the

night before, Humphries for some reason could not access the property. It was late so summoning the owner on his mobile phone was going to be a last resort.

With his concern growing deeper and weighing up his options, his mood lifted when he spotted a woman inside the property. He explained his predicament and she told him she'd open the gate once inside the house. So she disappeared inside and Humphries waited for the gate to open. He waited, and waited, and waited and was starting to wonder whether she had forgotten about him. The gate simply wasn't opening so after what felt like an inordinate amount of time Humphries decided to take matters into his own hands.

He did not, however, arrive at this point without due consideration. This, after all, was Australia, which meant that his plan to scale the fence may be met with consequences that may not be immediately apparent.

Anyway, it had to be done. He walked back towards the street and measured a Brett Lee-like run-up to try to get enough elevation to drag himself up and over the wall. On his first attempt he fell short, and duly added a few yards to his run-up. This time he was able to reach over the wall, which gave him sufficient leverage to pull himself up to the top. Problem is that with that body position, he was never going to make a dignified descent. His belly, still laden with Tooheys, was going to scrape over the top of the wall. Soon enough, his descent was one in which he wholly yielded to gravity.

He landed with a thud, but soon rose to his feet. It was then, as he looked to his left, that he realised what the woman had meant earlier before she disappeared into the guesthouse. A gate on the side of the property – one that he was in fact well aware of – was standing wide open.

Absolute catastrophe

It was not the way Jean de Villiers and Gcobani Bobo wanted to spend the 2003 tournament, but at least they got to do things and see places.

Both had been injured in the build-up to the tournament but were invited to attend as part of the entertainment in SA Rugby's Boktown initiative in Australia. This meant the pair would have to spend much of their time at the Leederville Hotel where Boktown had been set up in Perth. It was a place where Springbok fans could gather and perhaps absorb some South African culture, whether they live in Perth or not.

Bobo is the intrepid kind. He has the nose to sniff out interesting places and on this occasion he discovered a bar in Perth that played kwaito. He loves his music and on one visit to that bar he noticed an attractive, voluptuous girl he felt he needed to have a word with. Not much later they were on their way to her place.

Around 8am the next day they were on the road again, she dropping him off at his hotel. Then suddenly ... Screech! The car came to a halt. She had driven over a cat. This is awful, he thought. They needed to get the stricken animal to a vet. So they climbed back into the car with the cat and headed off.

At the vet the doctor on duty could only do so much and, sadly, the cat had exhausted the eight other lives apparently available to it. The girl was distraught. They walked outside and, although she had been dropping him off when the accident had taken place, he couldn't just leave her side now. So there they were, standing next to her car, with him trying to console her. Almost on cue, a bus pulls up with tourists on board.

One of the passengers, who runs a South African firm, shouts in their direction: "Bobo, Bobo!" He keeps his head down as the tears roll onto his shoulder.

A nip in the air

Sydney has a humid, subtropical climate. Its coldest ever recorded temperature was in 1932 when the mercury dropped to 2.1° Celsius.

The city's weather is largely moderated by its proximity to the ocean. Why all this is relevant will soon become apparent.

One Friday, after I had written my preview and ubiquitous weekend features ahead of the Test at Stadium Australia, I met up with my mate Gavin Dingley for a sundowner near Circular Quay.

The weather was mild but because it was late afternoon and the banking district is almost always a little shady, long sleeves were pretty much the order of the day. By the time I arrived, Dingley was already seated and had someone with him.

"This is Graeme," said Dingley pointing to his friend.

"Pleased to meet you," Graeme said in a gruff voice.

He was wearing a dark coat and scarf. This wasn't Christchurch, so I thought it odd that he would be so layered up.

Dingley explained that he was still a rookie at the expat business but that Graeme had moved to Sydney some 18 years earlier. Graeme merely smiled and nodded in agreement. They had only just arrived at the Customs House Bar so the first round was yet to be ordered. Dingley got our order and made his way to the bar.

Graeme wasn't saying much so to avoid any oncoming awkward silence I figured I'd ask him about why he is so clothed up.

"You sound a bit rough, big night?" I enquired not so tentatively. Graeme smiled, leaned forward and lowered his scarf fractionally before saying in his gruff voice: "Throat cancer."

To this day I don't know why I ventured a reply: "Well, that's bad too."

Cubana ooh-la-la

Covering a long rugby tour – even a local one – can dull the senses. One day seamlessly blends into the next and writers have to guard against complacency and repetitiveness. You can even lose the ability the recognise the bleeding obvious.

Two weeks into the British and Irish Lions rugby tour of 2009 colleague Ken Borland trudged down Main Road in Newlands after the tourists narrowly beat Western Province in a midweek match. He was in the mood for "a quiet beer" (which loosely translates to: not a five-o'clocker) and wandered into Cubana situated close to the intersection where Newlands meets Claremont. As you'd expect, rugby revellers all dressed in Lions regalia numbered high among the patrons and Borland immediately felt in his element.

Even when he minds his own business, people are drawn to Borland and soon enough he was part of a conversation with a group of travelling supporters, who of course well outnumbered the locals. He took great pride in telling them that he was covering the tour for one of the globe's leading news agencies, which by extension pretty much made him an authority on most oval-ball matters in the republic. The beer kept flowing, greasing already easy-flowing conversation. Borland could not have been happier but something kept bugging him. One of the tourists intrigued him. He seemed a little different from the rest. Eventually our local hack could no longer contain his curiosity.

"Tell me, what is a bloke with an Antipodean accent doing among a group of Lion supporters?" The moment he asked the question his blood turned cold in the realisation that he was already armed with the answer. One of those moments when you wish you could drag those words straight back into your mouth, the reverse of a clown's handkerchief trick.

The response came like a dagger to the heart. "Mate, I'm Riki Flutey. I played tonight!" said the New Zealand born England and Lions inside centre.

What's in a name?

Before SA Rugby was run by bean counters our teams travelling abroad only did so after they said goodbye at an official function. Whether that was the Springbok team, the national under-23s, or the Sevens side, the coaches and players had to gather in the function room of some hotel where someone with a blazer got hold of a microphone.

It was thus that I found myself at the entrance of a function room at the Woodstock Holiday Inn on the eve of the Springbok Sevens team's departure to Hong Kong in 1995. To the left of the door was a table stacked with media guides containing short biographies with vital statistics of the squad's players and management.

Typically, back then, it would have a picture of the player

to the top left of the page, with information such as his date and place of birth, height, weight, where he matriculated, studied, when he made his debut, number of caps, and so on.

In some media guides there would also be deeply private information like favourite food, movie, marital status and occupation. Around the mid- to late-1990s it was uncanny how many players listed *Braveheart* as the favourite movie, with *Shawshank Redemption* getting honourable mention. Steak was often listed under favourite food, with pasta also cracking the nod.

The media guides were generally a little shoddily put together. They would typically be A4 size, held together by wiry black plastic thread through the pages to make up the spine of the book. The reproduction or quality of the printing was appalling, the black-and-white head-and-shoulders picture of the players little more than a dark smudge because it had been photocopied a thousand times. Of course, black players were more compromised because their images consigned them to a universally unrecognisable black blotch.

So, waiting idly at the Holiday Inn, I picked up one of the media guides and flipped through the pages, looking for nothing in particular. I was wasting time, hoping to catch a glimpse of a friendly face inside the room.

While scanning the pages, however, I noticed the name of Chelton April. Aah, I thought, I can finally get some clarification on the spelling of his first name. In some publications his first name is spelt "Chelton" and in others "Charlton". I now entered the room armed with a purpose.

It's not long before I spot April and head across. He's standing in a small group, so I apologise for interrupting and introduce myself. I look him earnestly in the eye and ask: "Can you please clear this up for me? The *Cape Times* writes your name as 'Charlton', while we at *The Argus* write it 'Chelton'. Is it 'Charlton' or 'Chelton'?"

He tilts his head quizzically and says: "I'm Nigel Witbooi."

Against my wishes, the earth doesn't open beneath me but I'm brave enough to ask: "Is that Witbooi with an 'i' or a 'y'?"

Loose forward and a hooker

Team managers almost always have a lot on their plate. Before the game turned professional, planning an itinerary, booking flights and accommodation, dealing with the press, sorting passports and accounting for luggage were part of the routine. In a different way, they continue to have a lot on their plate, even though logistics managers and staff dedicated to players' affairs have lightened the load.

Before the advent of professionalism, team managers also had to do a fair amount of mopping up. Players would get into trouble and it always fell to the manager to clean up the mess. For this service in the amateur days, they would get little more than a blazer and a tie.

Post isolation, however, Springbok team managers have had it a lot easier. Although it has retained a degree of troubleshooting, it's almost as if the role has become more ceremonial. There are perks though: they get a generous allowance, generally fly business class and have a suite booked in their name wherever the Boks rest their weary heads.

A couple of nights before a Test in Perth in 2004, team manager Arthob Petersen's room had the look and feel of a presidential suite. There was a birthday worth celebrating and the touring media had been invited there for sundowners and snacks. The suite was a corner unit with a balcony and wonderful late-afternoon vistas of Perth. His bathroom was fit for Liberace.

The Boks had made the Burswood Casino resort complex on the banks of the Swan River to the east of Perth's city centre their home for the week. The complex, which houses three hotels, is almost a self-contained village, with more than 30 restaurants and bars, as well as a night club. The Boks wouldn't need to go walkabout – everything seemed to be in place under one roof.

Petersen, who held the position of team manager between 1997 and 1999, and again between 2004 and 2006, returned to the post for the Springboks' end-of-year tour in 2008. On his early deployment, his relationship with Nick Mallett had been famously frosty. He got along better with Jake White, but like Mallett, White had an inherent distrust of the elected officials in blazers.

This gathering in his suite was perhaps an opportunity to help forge a better relationship with the media. Enough booze could grease those wheels.

After consuming some of what was on offer we left in the early evening and headed for the nearest elevator not knowing quite what to make of the gathering. We hadn't made any plans beyond Petersen's little soirée so were quite happy to chat away, in no rush to get downstairs. Two of us even took the opportunity to lounge on a couch conveniently facing the elevator doors. But our position proved rather awkward for a Springbok forward very much in off-duty mode. As the doors parted, the forward's face dropped when faced with four journalists. He would ordinarily wear a smile and shake hands, but his arm was around the waist of a high-heeled blonde, long of leg, short of dress. This was not going to be one of those occasions where he'd greet everyone – the clock was ticking.

"These guys are my friends," the loose forward offered sheepishly. "They are journalists."

Missing "that" try

As has been explained, getting to New Zealand is a bit of a trek. Imagine undertaking an almost day-long journey only to miss the most critical moment of the tour.

It was July 2008 and the Boks had just come off a 19–8 defeat at the hands of the All Blacks in Wellington. The teams were due to meet further south a week later on the occasion of the last Test to be played at Carisbrook in Dunedin.

Xola Ntshinga and his cameraman Russell Belter vacated their seats in the press box, made their way to the back of the stand and then downstairs towards the tunnel where they were due to flash post-match interviews.

The crowd was in high spirits as the All Blacks had been keeping the Boks at arm's length and looked set to hold on for victory.

They made the way to the tunnel but something felt amiss. They had not seen any action but it dawned on Ntshinga that the stadium had fallen quiet. He turned enthusiastically to Belter and shouted, "I think we've scored. I think we've scored," momentarily unaware how his voice cut through the silence as they emerged from the tunnel.

Sure enough, when they looked up at the scoreboard, the Boks had scored.

They made their way to the Bok bench for some clarification.

"What happened?" Ntshinga asked Bok backline replacement Peter Grant. "Ricky did what Ricky does," said a less-than-animated Grant.

Although the Boks held a small lead, they still had to protect it in the remaining minutes. Immediately, the All Blacks went on to the attack and Ntshinga expressed his concern to Grant. Typically calm, the Stormers flyhalf turned to Ntshinga and said, "Don't worry, we've got this."

The Boks held their defensive lines and held on for a historic 32–29 victory.

Back in the change room the celebrations were wild. Ntshinga and Belter were cautious not to disturb the sanctity of the place, hanging back in the doorway with a framed view of what was happening, change-room protocol dictating that they enter only when invited in.

Coach Peter de Villiers spotted them and extended an enthusiastic invite. The two managed to capture the mood but the moment was lost when the SA Rugby president Oregan Hoskins and another blazer entered the room.

His congratulatory address to the team served only to draw the energy from the room.

Scrub, scrub, scrub

I'm not sure whether it came about through bureaucratic bungling or his own negligence, but former Springbok centre Gcobani Bobo ended up with two passports.

Bobo had been on the end-of-year tour and his passport, he thinks, ended up in the possession of SA Rugby. He couldn't account for it, so had to apply for another one early the following year when he was due to tour with the Sharks in order to fill their Super Rugby commitments in Australasia.

He got that passport in time to embark on the five-week tour, but when the team was due to leave Auckland for Sydney there was a problem. The team's long-time manager Trevor Barnes asked Bobo to step aside – one of the immigration officers had detected a discrepancy. They had picked up the fact that two passports had been issued in Bobo's name and needed him to stay behind to have the matter cleared up.

This meant that the team would proceed to Sydney without Bobo and, once everything was sorted, he would fly to join them in Australia the following day. But because back then South African teams toured for five weeks, he had two large bags, which he then handed to teammate Cedric Mkhize. He would collect them from Mkhize once he got to Sydney.

So the team flew out without him and Bobo remained behind with no more than an overnight bag. One of the bags he had handed over to Mkhize contained only shoes. A whopping 20 pairs. "They included my boots," he tried to explain later.

Now, anyone who has flown into Australia will be aware of how strict customs officials are about contraband or foreign substances brought onto their island. No foodstuffs, especially biltong, or plants. Nothing that can contaminate their soil or waterways are allowed to pass through customs.

Mkhize's problem was that he was in possession of someone else's bags and would have to declare that on his arrivals card when the team touched down in Australia. The other issue was that once customs officials opened Bobo's bags they found that the majority of the shoes were dirty. If, as a rugby player, you travel from New Zealand to Australia you will more than likely have Kiwi soil on your boots collected from the mud island.

So it was that Mkhize was refused entry into Australia until the boots were cleaned. While he started cleaning the boots his team had cleared immigration and customs, unaware of the chore that had suddenly been sprung on the young wing. While he sat there scrubbing Bobo's boots, his teammates were on the bus awaiting his arrival. Even though they believed he was just mucking about and now running late, the bus simply couldn't leave without him.

When Mkhize eventually finished he made his way to the bus and had to walk down the aisle, the object of dagger looks and the odd snide remark.

Gcobani Bobo had a similar walk of shame. In fact, his was worse.

On a night out on Courtenay Place in Wellington on tour with the Sharks in 2005, the Springbok centre lost track of time. They were flying out early the following morning but Bobo and some teammates had bumped into some Hurricanes players, including the late Jerry Collins. They had a good night out and Bobo didn't think much of it when his teammates left. There were still Hurricanes players around so he stayed.

When the Hurricanes players warned him that it was time for him to go, he looked at his watch and figured he could stay for another hour. So that is what he did – until he saw two men in familiar-looking attire walk into the establishment.

Filled with dread, he immediately recognised the kit as the clothes his teammates wear when travelling. He put down his drink and made his way to the door. Sure enough, outside the bar was the Sharks' team bus. They came to pick him up en route to the airport.

"Please go, Dave!"

Way back when the Springboks and the travelling media were on, let's say, better terms, they would often find themselves occupying the same space late into the evening. Increasingly, however, the players' interactions with the media were stage managed and generally limited to press conferences, mixed zones, sponsors' get-togethers, charity events and the like.

Back in the 1990s it was different. A former SABC journalist was one of the more popular among the players. The journalist, you see, always had wheels, and because he and his cameraman had to lug vast loads of equipment wherever they went, they almost always rented a van or a people carrier to get the job done.

On one trip to France he had to ferry groups of Springboks to grab takeaways because the players had grown tired of French cuisine. On another trip he explored Paris and word got out that he was heading to a suburb where, let's just say, there were colourful lights and characters.

He agreed to give a couple of excited players a lift but was a little surprised to discover that a near team load had assembled at the pick-up point outside the hotel. He had to make three trips to get all the Boks to their desired destination. On one of the drop-off runs he stopped at a pick-up point of a different kind. He wound his window down and asked the lady on the nearby pavement: "Do you have a special price for my friend? It's his birthday."

The woman promptly stepped closer and put her hand through the window into the tight forward's lap. The birthday boy didn't see that coming.

"Dave, drive please. Please drive," he exclaimed as the journo, amid a fit of laughter, struggled to get the vehicle into first.

In the nick of time

When players trip up, it is often left to the support staff to do some last-minute scrambling. And when the Springboks lost 37–25 to Argentina for the first time on home soil in Durban in 2015 something happened before the match that perhaps served as a portent for the hosts.

Logistics manager JJ Fredericks noticed a player hovering close to him, clearly anxious. When asked what was wrong, the player whispered sheepishly: "I left my boots at the hotel."

Traffic to Kings Park on Test day, whether you approach it from the CBD or Umhlanga to the north, can be a nightmare. But it was an hour before kick-off, so Fredericks had to make a plan. To compound matters, the team was staying at the luxurious Beverly Hills Hotel in Umhlanga, which meant the journey to the grounds would take a little longer than if they were staying in town.

A call was made to the hotel and they promised to dispatch a driver. The plan was that when he got as close to the ground as he would be allowed by traffic officials, the driver would call Fredericks with his location. So when he got the call, Fredericks set off from the change rooms, across the B-fields, through a haze of braai smoke out past the Virgin Active and beyond to the point where the driver's progress had been arrested.

Thankfully, Fredericks, a former Currie Cup captain, was fit as a fiddle. When he got a call enquiring how far he was, he informed his colleague that the player had better do his warm-ups in his takkies.

And finally, six or so kilometres later, Fredericks arrived in time with two pairs of boots.

In 2009 a rookie prop made a terrible *blaps*. No, he didn't collapse a scrum – much worse. The Boks had just beaten Italy 32-10 in Udine and were due to fly from Italy to Ireland for the last match in their end-of-year tour.

Their luggage had been sent in advance to Dublin. The prop had, however, inadvertently put his passport in his suitcase so at the airport he informed the folk who could assist that he had no passport. He was told to go back to the hotel and calls were made to the liaison officer in Ireland, with instructions to open the player's bag and find the passport.

That player remained in Italy for two days before he could join the team in Dublin. But, as it turned out, the match he had played the previous week was to be his first and last for the Boks.

If things occasionally veer off script logistically in the Springbok camp, imagine how – with fewer resources – pear shaped they can go for the Emerging Boks. One player had a rather interesting tour with the team during the tournament they played in Romania in 2008.

The Emerging Boks played a mix of A-teams from top rugby-playing nations as well as full Test teams from developing countries. The team under coach Chester Williams, with Deon Davids as one of the assistants, won the tournament and the after-party was scheduled to take place at the team hotel. All the participating teams would gather for the bash.

The Emerging Bok players were told that their luggage was to be collected at 7am the following day. They were thus instructed to pack their bags before they left for the function as things might become a little hazy later in the evening or the next morning.

The company tasked with the transfer of the bags needed to verify that they had 30-odd bags and that the same number was dropped off at the airport. The bags were duly checked in and sent on their way. The team, however, was only due to depart in the afternoon, which meant that some in the touring party did not feel obligated to get some shut-eye during the hours you would normally do so.

As anticipated, the post-tournament party was a long, raucous affair, with some players only hitting the sack at around 7am and were able to sleep off their babbelas. They were only due to leave for the airport at 3pm, where they would board an Air France flight from Bucharest to Charles de Gaulle, Paris, for their connection to OR Tambo International.

All the players made it to the airport but then one, a centre, already aware of a potential problem, approached the team manager.

"I can't find my passport," he told the official, no doubt already in the grips of angst.

"Look harder," he was instructed.

The manager was already aware of the situation, however, because he already had all the other players' passports, except that of the player in question. It soon became clear, though, that the player had left his passport in his suitcase, which had been picked up earlier that morning, and was already well on its way to Johannesburg.

Fortunately, the airline handed the manager boarding passes for everyone in the tour party. The problem, though, was that even if the centre was able to board in Bucharest, he would not have been allowed on to the second Air France flight in Paris. This meant that there was no way the centre could fly. It would prove a logistical nightmare, and it was becoming increasingly clear he would have to stay behind and be put up for a few nights in a hotel.

Luckily for the centre, the South African ambassador to Romania got to hear of the predicament, and extended the offer for the player to be his guest at the official residence for a "few days" until the matter was resolved.

The bags meanwhile had arrived in Johannesburg before being sent on to SA Rugby's headquarters in Newlands. This caused a further delay, because it meant that the team manager had to get to Newlands to open the bag and locate the passport. It then had to be couriered back to Romania.

The "few days" the player was supposed to stay with the ambassador became two weeks.

Enough is enough

It's beer o'clock. I've written what I needed for the day and after three-and-a-half hours of frantic writing I need to take a stroll. I agree to meet colleagues Mike and Louis a couple of blocks up the road from my Darling Harbour hotel in Sydney.

They have a headstart on me, having arrived at the bar some 45 minutes before I'm set to go through the door. When I arrive they are just finishing a round and Louis offers to buy the next one. A few minutes later he places two drafts on the table before returning to the bar for his. We natter away about everything except the Springboks' upcoming match against the Wallabies at Stadium Australia.

Jake White is resting some of his big guns for this Tri-Nations tour. For Saturday's Test, in John Smit's absence, Bob Skinstad will wear the captain's armband, while Johan Muller, who a week later would become the Springboks' 53rd Test captain, would wear the No. 5 jersey with Victor Matfield also back home. Interestingly, Muller would be the fourth player to captain the Springboks that year.

Before long I stand to get a new round. I had walked in with a bit of a thirst and downed my first beer. Louis and Mike's glasses were around half full.

I ask the youngster behind the bar for three Tooheys lagers.

"Two Tooheys and a Tooheys Lite coming up," he says.

"No," I say. "Three Tooheys."

He says: "Two Tooheys and a Tooheys Lite for you."

I look at him curiously. "Why's that?"

"You've had enough, mate. It's either two Tooheys and one Lite or nothing for you."

At this point, Louis has caught wind of trouble brewing over the Tooheys.

He steps in. "What? Are you telling my friend he can only get a Tooheys Lite because you think he's had enough?"

"Yes," replies the cheeky youngster.

"What the hell! Are you serious?" Louis asks. The barman nods.

Louis's next action pretty much puts paid to our continued presence at the establishment. "Well, in that case, take this," he says, leaning forward and emptying the remaining beer in his glass over the counter and into the large ice compartment. It's the last thing the barman expected, but we know for sure he's going to summon the doorman, if the large fella hadn't already noticed the flare-up.

Meanwhile, Mike, having observed what has just transpired, raises his glass to his mouth and downs the remainder of his beer in anticipation of our imminent eviction.

Some ID please

Sunday Times sport writer Khanyiso Tshwaku says he loves beer and that when he travels to a country he has not visited, he likes to try the local amber.

He once described how relieved he was to board an Air New Zealand flight from Perth to Auckland. His travel arrangements had gone desperately pear shaped and he was just happy to be on the move again.

"The thirst levels were peaking and, I mean, I'm on a flight to the Land of the Long White Cloud and beer's free," he recalled flying to New Zealand for the first time.

Australia and New Zealand are usually strict when it comes to alcohol consumption, and that is especially so on their airlines. Larrikin behaviour will not be tolerated above the clouds.

"But here's the problem," Tshwaku would later explain. "I've looked like a 16-year-old for the past 16 years and from time to time I have to produce identification to enter bars and taverns. It was a chore then and remains a chore now but I've learnt to embrace my youthful looks," he said with no trace of vanity.

"Having watched a fair bit of New Zealand rugby growing up and remembering that the All Blacks were once sponsored by Steinlager, it had to be the beverage of choice. So when the hostess asked whether I'd like a drink I asked for Steinlager.

"Clearly she hadn't taken a good look at me and when she returned with the dumpie, she gave me a long, hard, examining look. I've had that look many times before and it's unfortunate that my big eyes tend to light up when a good-looking lady has that searching look. Then the question came. 'If you don't mind me asking, how old are you, sir?'

"'I'm 29, turning 30 next year,' I said while reaching for my passport and driver's licence at the same time.

"She looked at the documentation and I could immediately see her look of surprise.

"'Sorry about that,' she responded with more than just a chuckle as fellow passengers looked up to check this adult minor who had had the gall to order barley beverage.

"I then said: 'Please bring three more,' as my fellow passengers marvelled at the courage of real-life Benjamin Button."

By the time Tshwaku flew back a week later, after

witnessing a 57–0 All Blacks mauling of the Springboks in North Harbour, he had tried to cultivate as much facial hair as he could to avoid being asked the same question.

Presidential treatment

Journalists flying cattle class aren't the only ones who fall foul of the moods of alcohol servers Down Under.

As SA Rugby representative on the Springboks' first Rugby Championship tour of Australasia in 2012, president Mark Alexander makes his way back to the team hotel after the Test in Perth. The Boks have lost 26–19, with Bryan Habana the only Springbok try scorer on that occasion. Frans Steyn banged over two penalties, as did Morné Steyn, but it wasn't enough to beat the Australians in a city that has become a bit of a fortress for the Wallabies.

Miffed at the result, Alexander decides to attend the press conference. The Boks failed to win their last two away matches. They had drawn with Argentina in Mendoza two weeks earlier.

He doesn't attend the post-match function and heads back into the city from the Subiaco Oval. It's around 8.30pm when he walks into the bar of the Pan Pacific Hotel. It's busy. There are lots of folk who have been to the game. There are almost as many blokes with familiar accents wearing green jackets as there are guys wearing gold jerseys with matching scarves. There are even South African journalists. Not having a single drink that day, Alexander heads for the bar counter. He orders a whisky, but is immediately told, "No, mate, you've had enough."

"Enough of what?" Alexander demands to know.

Incredulous, he looks around to see if anyone else has observed this. No, he's on his own. Knowing it's futile to argue with the snotkop behind the bar, he turns and heads for the exit and then the elevator.

Back in his room, he doesn't have to prove his sobriety to the door of his mini bar fridge.

Four

The Poffers

Poffers. This was the name bestowed on Springbok supporters by travelling rugby writers who often had to witness the loutish behaviour of their countrymen. The name was derived from the green puffy jackets Springbok supporters would typically wear. The Poffer phenomenon was particularly prevalent between 1992 and 2005. Fortunately, that culture has changed and South Africans have generally become better travellers. Also the emergence of the Gwijo Squad looks set to give the face of the average Springbok supporter a bit of a makeover.

In from the cold

THE IMPACT OF South Africa's sporting isolation reached far beyond the playing surface, or indeed the boardrooms. Isolation means exactly what it says. You are polarised, banished and left in the cold, with some distance between yourself and the warmth the masses generate.

White South Africa played and watched sport through the

prism of chest-beating nationalism, and being in the sporting wilderness meant that players, as well as the viewing public, developed a very narrow, if not parochial frame of reference.

The Springboks had not played a Test away from home since they beat the United States in surreal, if not outright bizarre, circumstances in Glenville, New York, in 1981. It had been a furtively arranged Test, played in secret following their deeply controversial three-Test tour of New Zealand. The Boks beat the Eagles 38–7 in front of 30 or so spectators, but they had to wait 11 years before they were to play another Test away from home.

So when the country was set on a political course that enabled the lifting of sporting barriers in 1992, South Africa were no longer the skunks of the international sporting community and, naturally, there was a craving to see the national team perform on foreign soil.

Soon our national teams became the darlings of the international sport and they were feted and often fawned over on foreign shores. This also meant that the folk who routinely sat in the stands at Loftus Versfeld, Ellis Park, Kings Park and Newlands were now free to travel and watch their revered team play in faraway lands.

While the Springboks quickly warmed to international travel, their fans took a while to familiarise themselves with the ways of the world. Travelling fans were almost exclusively made up of a very narrow sector of society, and white males would form tour groups and travel long distances to watch their beloved Green and Gold play. For them it wasn't just a chance to watch rugby; it presented the opportunity to break the shackles and abandon the inhibition that usually guides them at home.

There are two ways of describing the travelling Bok fan for the first decade or so post isolation. The first type would walk around Edinburgh, London, Paris or Sydney dazed, in a constant state of bewilderment. They reminded me of Jodie Foster's character in the movie *Nell*, in which a feral young girl comes face to face with people for the first time.

The other type is very different. They are the lager louts who upon arrival would set about town with the devil-may-care gusto of the Vikings of yore. It never ceased to amaze me how the character of a town or city would change on their arrival. From Sunday to Thursday midday you would get to experience the place for what it was, but then as the wave of Green and Gold arrived the locals would stop short of running for cover.

The Poffers would be instantly recognisable. They'd wear jeans or chinos and, because they invariably travel to a winter destination, a ubiquitous green puffed-up jacket. They may wear a different T-shirt or golf shirt but the Bok jacket and the jeans would be the go-to attire for the length of their stay.

Poffers on a plane

Earlier I described a hair-raising descent into Kai Tak, Hong Kong's decommissioned airport, when the pilot aborted the landing with the landing strip metres away.

The already restless Bok supporters on board were far from happy – by then they had consumed all the beer and brandy on our Cathay Pacific flight. They went through different stages on this 14-hour journey. Before and just after boarding, they were like Labradors on their first visit to the park. They cracked the odd joke, and glass, and there was to be no doubt the manne (the men) were going on tour.

The first few hours of the flight were like the opening few power-play overs in a T20 cricket match. "Make hay and go over the top because you can" was pretty much their mantra. Then, after the main meal they became more sedate. Like those middle overs in a one-day international where the scoring continues but now singles are almost reluctantly the order of the day. Some, of course, catch a second wind and up the ante, which has grave consequences for those in close proximity whether they are part of the increased intake or not.

By the time we completed two-thirds of the journey all the brandy and beer on board were either in pot bellies, in the toilets or, unavoidably, on the floor. The manne were tired and now keen to get off this flight, even if that objective was to lay their hands on more booze.

With the plane aborting touchdown due to the prevailing monsoon conditions, their angst grew deeper. The tournament was set to kick off in just a few hours, and besides, they were thirsty.

"Nee, fok," one piped up. "Jy land nou die ding!" (You land this thing now!) Others started muttering too until the flight attendant – the one who introduced her tea to my jeans – breezed down the aisle in their direction. I don't know what she told them but, bless her, they shut up. Even if Hong Kong was still in British hands, being banished to a Chinese jail should never be on your "to-do" list in Hong Kong.

I was determined to get my bags before the Poffers did, and anticipated a bun fight for taxis. The luggage carousel, however, failed to play ball and by the time I lugged my bag in the direction of customs they were all 20 or so metres in front of me.

I spotted the exit but there was no way of me slipping past them without breaking into a trot. Besides, I was hoping the customs official at the exit would politely pull some of the 15 or so aside for some interrogation. But the official in a dark uniform stood listless, and I had this nagging sense that not only was he going to let all these bastards through – because clearly they were in a group and here just to get more drunk – but that he would stop me.

Some of them even laughed at him with comments like, "Kyk die ou!" (Look at this guy!) as they pushed their trolleys past. Soon after a firm right hand close to my chest, rather than the guy's Cantonese, made me understand that I needed to stop. All I thought – but could not say – was, "I don't have the drugs."

Poffers in a lift

We're walking up Duke Street Arcade in Cardiff. It's November 2013, the Boks beat Wales 24–15 and we are going to have a drink.

I'm with my partner, Marcelle Gordon, and "Grote".

Earlier in the week, Grote and I had agreed to return to the bar where the owner Jeff made some interesting promises.

I told Marcelle about what Jeff had promised and even she was curious. But as we get closer to the entrance of the establishment, she opts out.

"Nah, you guys continue. I'm gonna head back to the hotel."

Now we feel a little awkward because what if what Jeff promised is true?

"No, come up with us," Grote tries to persuade her.

"Nah, it's okay. Enjoy," she says before we kiss goodbye and she walks the short distance to the top of the arcade before turning into Duke Street towards the Holiday Inn.

It's a short walk back to the hotel, but she cannot believe the number of people who appear to have committed body and soul to alcohol that afternoon. It's not even 9pm and she spots a father and son keeping each other upright.

I had warned her about Cardiff and the enduring devotion of the Welsh to have a good time over match weekend. Two nights earlier we had just finished supper when a taxi, the London variety in shape and colour, stopped next to us. Out poured four young women in various stages of pouring out of their dress. They could barely stand up straight and squabbled about where to go first. It was like a scene out of *The Valleys* but it was only 8.30pm so they had enough time to smile at a few doormen.

Marcelle reaches the hotel teeming with rugby revellers – it matters little that Wales lost – and passes a Guinness-branded bus that is rather strategically parked outside the hotel and then walks into the lobby.

People everywhere. Obviously the party has spilled over from the bar. Dressed in a black coat and beanie, she zigzags through the human traffic to the lift and thankfully no one else is going up. Then, just as the doors are about to close, a hand attached to an arm covered by a sleeve on a Springbok jersey prevents it from doing so.

It is accompanied by, "Wag! Wag!" (Wait! Wait!) from one of the Bok supporter's mates.

There are four of them, two wearing puffy Springbok jackets, while the other two are armed only with the jersey, but they are all unmistakably Poffers. Their cheeks are red and mood cheerily boisterous. Clearly eschewing room service, they are all clutching McDonald's bags. As Marcelle moves into a corner at the back of the lift, there's an acknowledging nod of the head and she looks down as the lift goes up.

She's not in the mood for the small talk the blokes are engaging in.

"Ons het dit gemaak," (We made it) one of them feels the need to confirm.

"Dit was a lekker dag," (It was a nice day) another points out.

"Dis nog vroeg," (It's still early) a third remonstrates.

But then the lift goes quiet, as it almost always does.

Just as the silence is reaching that uncomfortable threshold, one of the manne, a bloke with a moustache, turns to Marcelle.

He leans towards her and says, "Aren't you scared of being in the lift with four big Souff Efrican men?"

As the lift goes "ping" on reaching their floor, Marcelle responds: "Ek is 'n meisie van die Kaap – julle moet eintlik bang wees vir my." (I'm a girl from the Cape – you guys should actually be scared of me.)

The bloke with the moustache is stunned and almost trips as he vacates the lift. His mates, already in throes of raucous laughter, have cause to raise the decibels

Poffers off a plane

All Blacks scrumhalf Justin Marshall used to own a bar in Christchurch. It was a big joint and usually busy. At the start of the week it was generally quieter but this was Thursday night and some weekend revellers had vacated the blocks early.

Fellow *Sunday Times* hack JJ Harmse and I figure the

place would probably be bursting at the seams the following night, so we decide we would give it a miss tomorrow and have one or two extra tonight.

The walk back to the hotel is about 10 minutes, some of it along the calming meander of the Avon River. It's quiet and there is hardly a soul. Then again, this is Christchurch and it's just about the middle of winter 2004.

As we reflect on another silly evening we hear voices in the distance. It's dark so sound holds sway over sight. The men are getting louder, which means they are getting nearer, heading our way. I suggest to JJ that it's probably a group of Poffers who have just landed.

When you travel to New Zealand from South Africa using the least inconvenient routing you would generally board a Qantas flight to Sydney. The Springboks used to know Qantas flight number QF64 as the one that departs Johannesburg in the evening and arrives around mid-afternoon in Sydney the next day. Lately, however, cost saving has meant that they fly into the northern hemisphere, to, say, Singapore for their connecting flight to New Zealand. They travelled that route to Wellington via Christchurch in 2019.

Depending on where you're headed in New Zealand, you face a three- or four-hour wait for your connecting flight in Sydney. That flight takes around three hours, which means you touch down after 11pm before you walk through border control and customs.

It is by now clear the men walking towards us are Poffers. We know this by what they are saying and wearing. The gentle, serene flow of the Avon makes way for loud Afrikaans, mostly delivered in four-lettered form.

I say to JJ, "Whatever happens, we'll stop talking in

Afrikaans when they get within earshot." At this stage the last thing I want is a meaningless conversation. JJ agrees.

They are now closing in, checking us out. I still find it curious that when two groups of men walk past each other at that time of the evening, there is always a lull in conversation as they pass. As they draw level, however, JJ breaks the silence.

"Julle manne lyk dors," (You guys look thirsty) he says.

They stop, bemused but happy. "Ja, natuurlik. Ons het fokken lank gevlieg," (Yes, of course. We flew for a fucking long time) says the one closest to us.

The bloke behind him, however, opts to escalate matters.

"Waar's die hoerhuis?" (Where's the whorehouse?)

Poffer off a train

As I may have mentioned, the French have their quirks. They tend to do things a little differently, and the English like nothing more than poking fun at them.

Why, for instance, would you start a rugby Test at 9pm? They tell us that's their way of maximising their television viewing audience, but it is a huge inconvenience to those who actually attend the match. Teams who play France are faced with this oddity and they hate it.

Teams tend to have a match-day routine that they try to stick to and in the case of the Springboks it would mostly be geared around a 5pm kick-off at home and 7.30am-ish when they are in Australasia. In Argentina they often have an afternoon kick-off slot.

The 9pm kick-off in Paris brings its challenges.

For writers it means there is time to finish feature articles for Sunday newspapers, you can shop, go sightseeing and you'll still have time to spare before embarking on the longish journey to Stade de France. For goodness' sake, you can probably fly to Nice, spend the day on the beach and be back in time for the kick-off.

So we had time to kill in the build-up to France's home Test against South Africa in 2013. The week had been hectic in anticipation of the last match of the end-of-season tour so sightseeing wasn't possible.

We would start our day in Montparnasse to the south of the main tourist attractions and work our way north.

We get off at Clémenceau metro station, which when you resurface at street level brings you onto the Champs Élysées, and check out some of the street art in the stalls that line the iconic boulevard. We then decide to walk up the Champs Élysées towards the Arc de Triomphe and as we pass the entrance to Clémenceau station a fresh wave of tourists emerges from below the street. Lots are wearing Springbok jerseys, no doubt many of them having started their journey in London at the crack of dawn.

One man in his early thirties, I guess, emerges with his mobile phone to his left ear. He tells the person on the other end of the line: "I don't know. Wait, I don't know. I'm on that big main road here." Turning to his left, he says: "There's a big square building up the road."

My partner and I resist the temptation to walk into the oncoming traffic.

Poffer at a pillar

The Springboks' win over England in the RWC quarterfinal in 1999 meant that the champions from 1991 and the reigning champions would clash in the semifinals as part of a glorious double-header weekend at Twickenham. Understandably, the Springbok supporters were in full voice and, now emboldened that their team could go all the way, more and more were streaming into London.

By then the Poffers had developed the habit of going to the hotel where the Springboks were staying and making a nuisance of themselves. Former Springbok scrumhalf Werner Swanepoel would often talk about how they'd encounter the Poffers in the lobby after having been out for dinner in the build-up to a Test.

Invariably the question would come, "Is julle manne reg vir Saterdag?" (Are you guys ready for Saturday?) There was really only one answer.

On this occasion in London in the build-up to the semifinals, there were South Africans everywhere and expectations hit the stratosphere. Places such as Shepherd's Bush and Covent Garden were awash with Green and Gold – not that the Australian gold Wallaby jersey was absent, of course.

I was assigned to write a colour piece for the Saturday publications in the then Independent Group capturing the mood before the two semifinals. Obviously it had to have a South African slant.

I took my research seriously and in Covent Garden I went from pub to pub trying to tap into the prevailing sentiment that Friday. It, of course, meant that whoever I was trying to interview would offer me a pint and although I managed to record lots of sentiment, it didn't necessarily mean it was fit for print.

I would dutifully press on until finally, with the deadline

and the limiting two-hour time difference weighing heavily on the back of my mind, head back to my hotel room to write. I got everything done, but I'm not sure the folk awaiting copy south of the Limpopo were happy with the long wait.

In the semis, Australia and South Africa were first up. It was a tension-filled match, every mistake accentuated by potential movement on the scoreboard.

Springbok flyhalf Jannie de Beer displayed nerves of steel converting a late penalty in which angle and distance were potential co-conspirators. It was, however, more than a touch ironic that the Wallabies' indomitable flyhalf Stephen Larkham would land a wonder drop goal that separated the teams before the ice-cool fullback Matt Burke converted a penalty to seal the Springboks' fate.

The Bok fans were crushed. The team too took it hard. Copious amounts of copy containing fallout and reaction got filed that evening. And when we finally stopped we agreed to meet some Kiwi journalists somewhere in Putney.

The restaurant was warm and cosy, but the most striking thing once we got to our table was the sheer glee that the Bok defeat had generated in the Kiwi ranks. They didn't rub it in, but they were just smug enough for you to know that they were smug. Kiwis are usually restrained and seldom go over the top, unless of course it is a fetcher flank.

For the South African media the Sunday too would be largely dedicated to writing about the Bok exit for the Monday papers, but we knew by the time we got to Twickenham for the second semifinal we could breathe easily. The pressure of having to file a tonne of copy had subsided slightly because the Boks were still destined to play the loser of the second semifinal between New Zealand and France, the teams who had met in the first ever RWC final in 1987.

France were the clear underdogs. New Zealand had swept all before them in the pool stages and even vanquished England by a considerable margin. They even took time out to travel to the Mediterranean for a mid-tournament break. Coach John Hart felt the team needed to be refreshed and that it would not compromise their momentum.

Although unbeaten in the pool stages, France laboured to victory against Canada and Fiji, before they beat Argentina for the right to play New Zealand in the last four. Given what we had experienced in that restaurant in Putney the night before, every score the French made in clawing their way back into the match was happily cheered by the South African media.

Once the Tricolores hit the front the Kiwi journalists were dumbfounded. It was like a train wreck unfolding in slow motion before their eyes and there was nothing they could do about it. In the biggest upset of the tournament, France prevailed 43–31 to extend the All Blacks' wait for another RWC title by at least another four years.

The South African fans, who comfortably outnumbered the French, were in high spirits. The Springboks' fiercest foes had also been removed from the challenge for the title. Life was sweet.

As we headed to an exit that would take us onto Whitton Road I noticed a man in black to my right, his head in his hands facing one of the stadium's giant pillars. He was about 10 metres away from the rush towards the exit and sobbing uncontrollably.

Just as I was thinking, "Ag shame", a Poffer walking in front of me veered off course straight to the Kiwi. Of course, the move captured our attention but what followed wasn't entirely surprising. The South African raised his right hand and slapped the unsuspecting Kiwi on the back: "Ag nee, ou maat. Môre is nog 'n dag." (Ah no, mate, tomorrow's another day.)

Five
After Midnight

As the name suggests, the events that unfold deep into the night have nothing to do with JJ Cale's big hit.

Late-night craving

WE'RE HEADING BACK. By Courtenay Place's standard, we've had an average night. Then again, it's the middle of Test week in Wellington 2010 – the place will spring to life in less than 24 hours.

The walk up Courtenay Place is an experience and having company makes it even more fun. It's never dull and my colleagues Ken Borland and JJ Harmse are familiar with the sights and sounds.

As we pass a restaurant with a suggestion of elegance, our attention is drawn to the broad-shouldered men occupying space just inside the door. They're having a right royal time and at least two of them think it's a good idea to take turns to put each other in a headlock. Ordinarily, we'd just press on, but the idea of writing a story later that day involving members of the Springbok coaching staff Os du Randt or Dick Muir crashing through glass doors wasn't particularly appealing.

"If we walk in we'd defuse the situation," one of us sagely suggests. Sounds like a plan, but we aren't sure how we'll be received once we walk through those doors. The other option is to leave the scene and let nature take its course. We feel like wildlife photographers observing lions happening upon an African wild dog and her litter.

It's a moral dilemma. Do we leave them in their natural habitat or do we do something that will make everyone's life a little easier the next day? Besides, one more beer wouldn't hurt... So we head for the door, albeit with a little trepidation.

The two are ecstatic to see us and soon we too are in a headlock. We should really have seen that coming, but that was just them showing affection.

They are in the company of three other fellas, one of whom is former All Blacks No. 8 and erstwhile Sky commentator Murray Mexted. All are in a festive mood. It's the Springboks' day off and Os and Dick have had a long day playing golf, as the Springboks often do on their day off, which is usually a Wednesday.

It is all quite raucous, but the restaurant is just about empty and nobody is too bothered by the, in this case, boysterous group.

Ken is engaged in deep conversation by Mexted and it isn't clear whether he needs a wingman or a proper intervention. JJ and I can't do much. Dick and Os command our attention. Ken, buddy, I think to myself, you're on your own.

Eventually, it is time to go. The place is closing and

the job we came to do is effectively done. Mexted and his mates go their own way while we head up Courtenay Place to our respective hotels. Where Courtenay Place forms an intersection with Taranaki Street, Os, Dick and JJ turn right while Ken and I keep going straight.

The rest of the tale is recounted the following day. The trio that had turned right got to an intersection where two of them needed to turn left towards the former Duxton Hotel, later called the Amora. Problem was that diagonally across the road there is a BP garage with a McDonald's attached to it. Os recognised the big M sign and duly crossed the street. Dick and JJ, perhaps out of a sense of duty, followed.

Os placed an order for quarterpounders that ran into double digits. At first the cashier wasn't too surprised. Soon, however, he was left aghast that the order was just for Os.

Back to the scene of the crime

Even more than in Perth, it always feels as if the local constabulary is looking over you in Queensland. If you spit in the street, or discard litter, you can expect a tap on the shoulder.

You watch your step, and don't appear as if you've had one too many.

You can get into trouble for entering a bar after being asked to leave earlier. You can also get into trouble for entering a bar if you were asked to leave another within close proximity.

Former All Blacks scrumhalf Jimmy Cowan got into hot water while on tour with the Junior All Blacks when, during his late-night walkabout, he blundered back into the bar from where he'd been ejected. Team management took a dim view once the incident surfaced on their radar and sent the scrumhalf back home over the Tasman. Despite the strict policing, the locals still behave like larrikins. The bars close early, however, which means your only viable alternatives to grabbing a beer is at the casino or a strip joint, which of course holds its own peril.

On one trip a hack left the historic bar at the Victory Hotel with his thirst not quite quenched, the smell of beer luring him down some steps to a strip joint that happened to be on the route back to his hotel. He claims he did not see the sign until he stumbled upon it. At this point, I need to point out that he's quite a talkative fella, which means this story was shared generously on tour.

He duly paid his entry fee at the cubicle adjacent to the entrance, got a stamp on his wrist, greeted the doorman and went inside. He got his beer and seemed quite content as he surveyed the dimly lit premises. It wasn't long, though, before a young lady with curly blonde hair sidled up. Soon her subtle advances made way for the more brazen suggestion of a lap dance in a private suite and although this service was a little steep in rand terms his right hand locked into her left as she led him to a back room.

The private suite was apparently not as private as he thought it would be. The room, which was even darker than the open-plan bar and stage area, basically had room dividers that broke the space up into four or five areas of laidback relaxation.

Once he was sitting back, the woman was as chatty as he was. He couldn't place her accent and yielded to his curiosity. She was American but had done a bit of travelling and was now dancing to get enough money to complete her studies.

When he told us the story the next day there was more rolling of the eyes than when teenagers get picked up at school. Apparently, he and the blonde were getting on like a house on fire and she seemed genuinely interested in what he did for a living. He told her his name was Dave and we sniggered when he shared the news. "You don't look like a Dave," a cameraman said bluntly, in the way only a cameraman can. Nonetheless, he articulated exactly what we were all thinking.

Anyway, Goldilocks was grinding away and although "Dave" was enjoying every minute of it, he thought he'd help her along while channelling one of his fetishes. "Dave", you see, loves feet and administering foot rubs counts among his guilty pleasures.

But touching dancers is, of course, strictly prohibited. With her facing him, he asked her if he could rub her feet. She explained that it would be great but that the controller, who is in an elevated cubicle to their right next to the entrance, might notice.

"Dave" was rather in the moment and figured he'd take his chances with distance and poor visibility as allies. He stretched his arms and furtively placed his fingers on the bridge of her feet. Then he placed his thumbs on the other side of her feet and gently started rubbing.

She looked a little bemused by this initially, "Dave" told us the next day, but she soon wore a smile as wide as his. He was sinking his thumbs deeper into the soft tissue at the bottom of her one foot and Goldilocks was warming to the occasion – which essentially meant she was grinding on top of him with more vigour. The harder "Dave" sank his thumbs into the soft tissue under her foot, the more purposefully Goldilocks moved on top of him. By the time the controller leaned into a microphone to declare time was up Goldilocks was groaning softly, her back arched.

She quickly suggested "Dave" reload, err, pay for a second dance. Realising, however, that their relationship had rapidly advanced, he had no qualms telling her that the state of the South African economy and the ailing rand precluded such excess.

Back in the bar he bought her a drink, and had a beer before saying "cheers".

The following night he returned to the "Vic", this time accompanied by other members of the travelling troupe. As last round was called and with the prospect of finding another bar door open rapidly diminishing, "Dave" declared cheerily, "I know a place."

The men drank up and dutifully followed "Dave" down a street close to the Elizabeth Mall. Suddenly "Dave" took a sharp left down some stairs. At the foot of the stairs was a cubicle where a girl with dark hair was seated. Next to her, however, was a girl with curly blonde hair whose eyes lit up as she looked up. "HE'S BACK!" she exclaimed. "I can't believe it, he's back!"

"Let me show you Paris"

Dinner is spectacular. Marcelle and I have ventured into Saint Germain and found a bistro where we've tucked into la langue de boeuf (beef tongue) and confit de canard (duck confit) among other delights.

Two members of the media join us later. One of our dinner companions enquires about the size of the steaks while his colleague tries in vain to locate the section on the menu dedicated to burgers.

We take a taxi back to Montparnasse where we all disembark outside their hotel. I forget my beanie in the taxi and that really pisses me off.

Marcelle and I cross the road for the 150-metre walk to our hotel. It's around 11pm and there is a light drizzle. There is hardly anyone on the street. As we get to within 50 metres of the hotel my attention is drawn to a bloke wearing a rain jacket with a hoodie drifting slightly into our path.

He suddenly lunges at us, but the initial shock soon makes way for relief. We recognise him as Damian Dussault, a local player agent. He has had dinner with Springbok prop Gurthrö Steenkamp, one of the South African players he represents.

"Don't tell me you are going to bed already?" Damian teases. I tell him we have to head back because I have to be up early for a live telephone interview with a South African television channel.

He then throws down the gauntlet. "Do you really want to go to bed, or shall I show you Paris?"

Now, let me just say, that is not the kind of offer you get every day. So we hail a taxi, head back in the general direction of where we had dinner and hit the back streets of Saint Germain. We find ourselves at a place called Le Pousse Au Crime and with a name like that who wasn't going to go in? The doors are shut but Damian is confident we can get in. He knocks, says something to the person who opens the door and we're in.

The bar area looks dingy and is just about empty and we head for the back, an area clearly designated for dancing. One drink becomes two, then three and so on. More people trickle in and the atmosphere is transformed.

Damian explains that, back in the day, the place used to be frequented by players from Paris's elite clubs Stade Francais and Racing Metro. They only occasionally visit now.

We drop anchor in Le Pousse Au Crime for a few hours before Damian reckons it's time to go. We then head back through the bar that was empty earlier and now you can barely see the walls. Back on the street we don't walk far before we're heading through the doors of The Bedford Arms. The lights are bright and the place is packed.

We snake our way to the bar and there we remain for some time. By the time we leave the light is starting to change. It's that late, or early. Heading out, we're all ravenous. Damian seems to know exactly where to go and soon enough he tucks into a steak tartar and I slice into a T-bone. It's after five and this calls for desperate measures.

I keep reminding Damian that we need to get a move-on because I have that crossing at 6.45am, but eventually we finish and are back into a taxi headed for Montparnasse. I figure it is going to be touch and go whether I get to the room before the studio calls.

Then my phone rings. They've called five minutes earlier than agreed and we are still a block or so from the hotel. I ask Damian to order the driver to stop. He takes his time. The plan now is to do the crossing while I'm walking the last bit back to the hotel.

And then, even sooner than I thought, I'm live. Thankfully, I had prepared for the crossing the day before so I knew what needed to be said. Problem is that I still had to deliver it in a clear, coherent way and there is also the small matter of Paris rush-hour traffic metres away.

There is the odd verbal stumble but I press on and all is fine. Eventually, though, the presenter back in Joburg enquires, "Liam, it sounds awfully noisy, whereabouts are you?"

Oh dear, don't freeze now, I remember thinking. "The French are an odd lot, Alistair," I start my reply. "Why this hotel would have a fire-alarm drill at this early hour is beyond me."

Dancing queens

The objective is to have a sundowner, or two, so when Pub Liverpool comes into view it piques our interest. An English pub in rural Argentina has to be checked out. Besides, its says "Liverpool" so some of us don't need an invitation.

Pub Liverpool looks and sounds as English as they come. The hits keep coming and a little uncannily I predict the next two songs in the compilation that booms through the speakers. I think I may have heard the exact compilation disc before.

It is hard to leave but our time in Pub Liverpool is up. While some in our group drift off to their accommodation, five of us opt for a slow stroll in search of food. We don't get very far. Diagonally across the road from Pub Liverpool is a curious-looking place. We can hear music and muted cheers, but we can't see anything because posters on the windows visually insulate the premises. There is a narrow alley that we presume leads to the door, but we are not sure about whether we should proceed. It sounds interesting, but is there a cover charge and will they have food? So many questions.

Our curiosity gets the better of us. Besides, once we're at the door, if we decide we don't like the place we can move on.

We get to the door that is shut, but soon enough it opens. The doormen smile as if they've been waiting for us for weeks and wave us in. The place is packed. Up ahead to the left is a stage with a catwalk. It's dark but we notice a flurry of activity in the distance next to the stage. A couple of folk are being unseated by the staff and ordered to the side.

They wave us in and by now we're getting the sense that everyone in the establishment is looking at us. We can't bail out now, it would look silly. So we proceed down to our table where other staff members eagerly await us. Our table is next to the stage, at the start of the catwalk. At least two blokes in our party seem a little hesitant. One keeps saying: "What *is* this?"

The rest of us ignore him. There is a woman on stage wearing a frightening amount of make-up. She is also wearing a dress that sparkles and only when I notice the feathers in her right hand does it dawn on me what we are in for. She is eyeing us. It is not every day that five men walk into an establishment in this town and three of them are black.

She continues with her routine, which involves singing and talking, mostly engaging those close to her. "She" then welcomes the other drag queens on stage and by now our unease has subsided. Eventually the host is back on and she's looking our way. The unease returns.

By now she knows we are from the southern tip of Africa. The Springboks are in Mendoza; surely we had to be South African. She summons one of us up. It's the bloke with the longest hair.

First she talks to him suggestively. He seems relaxed enough. Then she seats him on a chair and dances suggestively around him. The audience goes wild.

Thank goodness he's a good sport, otherwise she would have had more of us up there. We're having a good laugh on this raucous night, but where's our food?

Bring me a bucket

It's early in the week, and relatively early in the evening when my mate Grote and I make our way back to our respective hotels. We have had a meal but don't see the point of hanging around as town is quiet and the mild drizzle provides further inspiration for bed.

Later in the week the Boks are set to play the first match of their 2013 end-of-year tour of Europe against Wales, but that seems far off as we head up Duke Street Arcade in the direction of Cardiff Castle. At the top of the pedestrian mall I would generally turn left to my hotel while Grote would turn right to his accommodation that boasts an additional star.

We'll have a couple of early nights because Cardiff, whether you like it or, can be quite manic on the weekend. We know that later in the week the pedestrian mall we have just walked up will take a beating from thousands of feet eager to get to the next drinking hole.

Of all the major cities that host rugby Tests, Cardiff springs to life on weekends like no other. On Test-match weekend supporters descend on the capital from the valleys to help create a party atmosphere that is a real eye opener for the uninitiated. The young bucks are as ready for their next drink as their next fist pump, while the average lass spills as much from her glass as she does from her dress.

We are nearing the top of the mall and we notice some activity near a bar entrance to our left. There are four guys and one of them breaks from the group and heads our way with what looks like a pamphlet. He greets us well before he reaches us.

"We have this amazing offer," he continues.

Sceptically we turn to him, "Nah, dude, we're not interested."

"You boys not from here?" he drags on the conversation by stating the bleeding obvious.

"But check this deal," he says, pointing to the pamphlet.

Essentially the establishment he represents is offering a bucket of beer (six bottles) for £15. We're still not interested, but assure him we'll be back later in the week to check the place out. He's persistent, though, on account of it still being early and six Heinekens for 15 quid is a good deal.

Soon a red rope is lifted and we tip toe over a short and by now soaking red carpet. The establishment is upstairs, to the right of a sign that reads "Floyds". We enter and the bar counter is conveniently positioned immediately to our left while the rest of the joint opens up to our right. There are fewer than 10 people in the place but there's a girl on the dance floor that should be in a Travolta movie.

We place our order for a bucket and self-deprecatingly laugh about being talked into coming into this dingy joint. The beer is cold and the place looks like it might have potential later in the week. Now, however, we are just keen to finish up and head off.

Behind the bar in the corner to the left a rather big fella is eyeing us. In the poorly lit bar we can just about make out his silhouette. He suddenly gets up and heads our way.

"Where you fellas from?" he enquires.

He is thrilled when we tell him we're from the southern tip

of Africa. Jeff is from West Africa but his mother apparently spent a lot of time in South Africa. He's ecstatic to have us in his establishment.

The Heineken is falling a bit easier. Jeff is keen to see us later in the week. We tell him we are well aware of what Cardiff is like on Test-match weekends, but what he says next by way of personal endorsement has us off our chairs.

"Mate, you come here on Friday night," he says, pointing towards the dance floor. "You'll see Cardiff's dirtiest pussy, right here."

A "tight five" go walkabout

It's week three of a long end-of-year tour and the boys are getting restless. There are two more weeks to go after this – one in London and one back in Cardiff for what now feels like a meaningless match against the Barbarians that will signal the end of the 2000 season. This week, however, it is Wales who commands the Boks' attention with a Springbok midweek team set for duty against Wales A before the Test at the then Millennium Stadium on Saturday.

As you can imagine, it is a busy travelling group. Travel arrangements have been manic but coach Harry Viljoen is keen for the players to integrate to give the younger players a taste of what it is like in the build-up to a Test. That also means that there are going to be young men who play their midweek match and don't have much to do for the remainder of the week and, in a rugby-mad city like Cardiff, if you'll pardon the expression, it is like shooting fish in a barrel.

Because they are effectively writing about two teams, the writers are never short of copy, but that also means that they build up a thirst through the excessive bashing of their keyboards.

Two writers who had typed their finger tips to a pulp find themselves in the Aussie theme bar on a walkabout late one evening. There are some Bok players around too. When closing time arrives the scribes head for the door at about the same time a couple of Boks do the same.

They have company.

One has each arm around a young lady – and he's not seeing them to a taxi.

Once they are beyond the doorman, there is a bit of small talk.

"Welsh girls are really lovely," the one with his arms spread tells the scribes. There are grins all round. He follows that up with: "Ons gaan nou lekker naai." (We're gonna have a good fuck.)

They then walk in formation, back to the team hotel.

The two scribes, still having a good chuckle, head off to their accommodation.

Later in the week it emerges that some Springbok players are in hot water because a used condom had been found in the pocket of a pool table in their hotel team room. The players are censured for a serious breach of team protocol, and the story makes it onto the news pages of a South African newspaper, which means that other papers follow suit. The incident has coach Harry Viljoen incensed.

We were left wondering, however, what exactly the players were punished for. Could their infraction only have been the improper disposal of a condom?

Dreaded moment

The Boks are in Edinburgh, and the mood needs to lift. They started their four-match tour of the United Kingdom, Ireland and Argentina with a narrow win over Wales, before coming up short against Ireland and England. In fact, against England they were well outplayed, but they now have an opportunity to balance the tour book against Scotland.

It's early in the week and hooker Hanyani Shimange and centre Gcobani Bobo bump into mates they know from Rondebosch. There are lots of laughs and, in some cases, lager. They are in a rather swanky establishment with thick carpets and ornate decorations.

Bobo is handed a drink that he later describes as "lukewarm water". He pretends to drink it but the contents of the glass flies over his shoulder – and the moment he does that he realises the folly of his ways. He is straight in the eye line of the bouncer who, although some distance away, has spotted the infraction.

The bouncer moves in but, sensing his guilt, Bobo nudges towards the door, which he is duly shown. He wants his teammate to join him in the freezing cold but Shimange is a smart hooker.

With no apparent way back in, Bobo is thrown a lifeline. His roommate Solly Tyibilika, who is to make his Test debut that Saturday, walks up. Bobo edges back to the door, and asks to be let in but the bouncer refuses. Bobo then points to his fellow dreadlocked teammate, dressed more or less the same way, and says, "It was him."

The bouncer responds with, "The fact that you know it was him is enough to keep you out."

That Bobo is the elder statesman in their roommate set-up is in itself interesting. He is a colourful character and at times peril finds him even when he is minding his own business. On a tour to Australia he and Shimange decided to rent surf boards. Clearly, their Cape Town background gave them some courage despite the fact that neither of them had surfed before.

They paddled out into the Pacific Ocean and were so proficient at doing it that when they turned around the folk on the beach appeared like dots. They frantically tried to paddle back, but the current was too strong. At some point Bobo fell off his board and was struggling to clamber back on. "Help a brother!" he begged Shimange, who was having his own trouble staying on his board.

Thankfully both eventually made it back to shore.

The day before the Test against Scotland in which Tyibilika is supposed to make his debut, the flank is naturally a little nervous. It's early evening and Tyibilika decides to have a cigarette to calm his nerves. He is hardly two puffs in when there's a knock on the door.

Bobo opens and it is coach Jake White who is there to check in on the following day's debutant and to make sure all is okay. With the door not fully open yet, Tyibilika rushes to the bathroom vainly swinging his arms followed by a trail of smoke.

Bobo says to White: "I'm just off to the physio. Solly's inside."

Whiskey or whisky?

End-of-year tours have a habit of throwing you off your routine. If you're into fitness and like running, you are likely to encounter days when venturing outside for that simply isn't an option.

Your eating and drinking habits suffer too. You get accustomed to restaurant food, and in Europe you are more likely to drink pints than brandy or whisky – mostly for economic reasons, because the rand routinely takes a pounding.

It dawned on me in Edinburgh on the end-of-year tour of Europe in 2013 that scribes rarely deviate from their set ways on tour. The guys are more likely to drink lager and occasionally a bitter while in the United Kingdom, but I thought it might be a good idea to break routine and try out a whisky bar.

It wasn't nearly as hard a sell as I thought it might be and after dinner four of us walk through the door of the Albanach on High Street. It is a glorious place if you appreciate whisky, but it can also be a little intimidating. The whisky menu is vast. Not just because of the number of whiskies they list, but also the detailed descriptions on the menu.

We read the small print. The font size is ridiculously small and increasingly it feels like we are going to blind taste. We all settle on our choices and one after the other our whiskies arrive. Some are easier on the palate than others but after five or so each we are ready to go.

We leave and get back onto the Royal Mile satisfied that we have done our bit to absorb a bit of the local culture.

Now we're heading to a bar we have been to a couple of

times earlier in the week: the Royal Mile Tavern, which is also desperately close to the hotel where the Boks are staying. I take orders for a round.

My companions all opt to revert to lager. I decide to stick to what I've been having but crucially whiskey and not whisky. I place the order and the barman pulls the three pints of lager, leaving the whiskey for last. He might have poured the Jameson while one of the pints is filling the glass, I think to myself.

Eventually he gets to it. He pours the Jameson, turns around in a mild huff and places the glass with a thud in front of me, saying: "And it's a fucking disgrace!"

Bobo and Jerry

Gcobani Bobo hits the streets of Dunedin with other members of the Springbok touring party. He's with some teammates but there is also a member of management who knows his way around town, and most bars where the Boks have toured.

Dunedin is a university town and its surrounds are agricultural. In fact, on your trip from the airport you'd be forgiven for thinking you're deep in the Welsh countryside.

Bobo and his group walk into a bar and his face lights up because there are some familiar faces. All Blacks flank Jerry Collins is there, as is Highlanders and later Samoa centre Seilala Mapusua. They end up having a complete blast, Bobo with the Kiwis, and eventually make a weary retreat to their hotel.

For the Test against the All Blacks at Carisbrook later that week Bobo gets picked at inside centre with the deeply comforting pressure of Louis Koen and Jorrie Muller either side of him.

"The one thing I remember most about that Test is Jerry Collins eyeing me," Bobo recalls. "Whenever he got the ball he would barrel straight down my channel. We had that big night out and they had John Mitchell as their coach and they obviously figured I was going to be a weakness in defence.

"I kept making tackles, however, and after a while he stopped running at me," says Bobo, his relief still palpable years later.

Six
Pressing Matters

Press conferences are largely dreary affairs. Generally, the folk speaking into the microphones don't want to be there, and the people on the other side feel they could have spent their time more productively. When things drift off script, however, it can be wonderfully entertaining.

Coaches' quirks

FOR SOME A SCOURGE, for others a primary source, the press conference has long established itself as the world's porthole to professional sport.

It is the platform from which in-demand sports try to transmit their sterilised, even manicured message into the public domain. I often think of the Crocodile Harris hit "Give Me the Good News" when I walk into a press conference because for those facing the microphones it is all about their message and not about the most burning issue. It is as soulless as an empty Southern Comfort bottle.

Of course, for sports writers it is all about "what's news". It means these gatherings of the performers and the press (at least for the senior writers) have become a delicate dance between what the former knows and how it can potentially be coaxed from them.

Imperceptible to many, generally there is a beat and a rhythm to every press conference. It is, however, easily disturbed. At times, when an awkward question needs to be asked, it is usually reserved for the tail end of the gathering. All too often, however, some young buck barely out of cadet school jumps in with a question that puts the coach on the back foot and before we know it the coach is out the door. A typical example would be: "You only have three black players in your starting line-up …" or "Your team has received five yellow cards in as many matches …"

Very often coaches themselves are coached before they walk through the door. As much as we want to know why a player was dropped, coaches are much more inclined to extol the virtues of the new guy coming in. Some coaches, however, are quite happy to tango, and at times tangle, with writers. Some deliver explanations with great glee to an audience they believe is in desperate need of schooling.

Every coach has his quips and quirks, and indeed his go-to words or phrases.

Former All Blacks guru Graham Henry, a former headmaster, would address the media as if he had just called us to assembly. He often finished an answer by turning it into a question.

"Richie McCaw is a captain in the finest tradition of All Blacks rugby, isn't he?" Henry might say.

If a question was clumsily framed Henry would turn on

The Hong Kong Sevens is a celebration every rugby nut should attend at least once. It is wonderfully festive. This was during the 1996 tournament in the Happy Valley Stadium.

It was during the 1999 Rugby World Cup that I got to learn the shortcuts in Paris from friend and colleague Barney Spender, who has an enduring love for the French capital.

The rolling hills that form part of the Dolce Fregate lay-out on the Côte d'Azur. The Boks stayed there in 2002.

Our work here is done. Some of my travel companions in 2002 – at the back with me from left Simnikiwe Xabanisa, Tertius Pickardt and Hennie Brandt. In front are Mike Greenaway and Louis de Villiers.

The build-up to that glorious Rugby World Cup quarter-final in Paris in 1999 where Jannie de Beer sent England packing.

I never get tired of the views Sydney has to offer. When he got older, Wallaby scrumhalf George Gregan's slow looping pass was also called the Harbour Bridge.

Brothers in arms – in 2012 with from left Pieter Jordaan, Craig Lewis and Vata Ngobeni, against the eastern slopes of the Andes.

"Ons gaan nou braai" – the Argentinean asado (braai) is a thing of beauty. They take their meat very seriously. We were invited on the eve of the 2012 Test against Argentina in Mendoza.

Some of the women who hounded us for pictures outside Mendoza in the Andes in 2012.

My colleague Vata Ngobeni thought he was ready for Taupo, but the New Zealand lake town was not so welcoming.

Vata Ngobeni and the Maori Chief Timi Te Heuheu, who wanted to make nice after Vata's rough treatment in Taupo.

Abrakebabra – at this kebab joint in Wellington in New Zealand, the portions are massive. It's a shame they close so early. Across the ditch in Sydney we discovered a wonderful hole in the wall next to a late-night hangout called Scruffy Murphy's on Goulburn Street. Its kebabs are a life saver, and it's even better when the owner says: "Mate, your money's no good here."

The team from the south at the Colin Elsey Shield media match. Soundly beat and beaten, we were in no state to engage in such physical exertion.

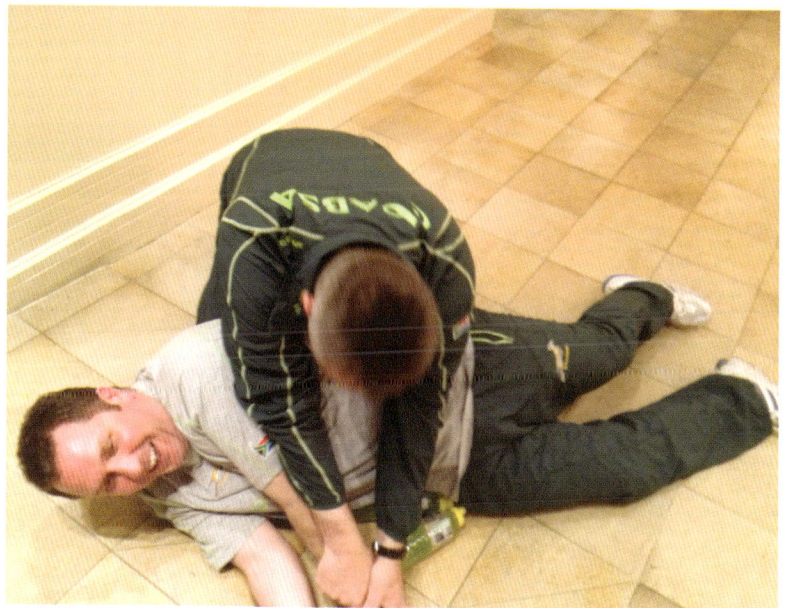

Bok coach Heyneke Meyer shows us the rucking technique – with media manager De Jongh Borchardt as prop – he expects from his team during a game against the Wallabies in Perth in 2012.

Hang'em high. I still don't know how I agreed to this. That's me dangling from the Auckland Harbour Bridge in New Zealand in 2012. I was the last of us to jump, which meant I went through more anguish.

Coffee gets me going in the morning. This is a quaint little shop near the hotel the Boks seem to prefer in Wellington, New Zealand. It's also a much-underrated venue to pick up the day's gossip.

The Welsh Male Voice Choir is a pre-match institution in Cardiff. This is 2013.

Working on the move in 2013 en route from Cardiff to Manchester before getting onto the TransPennine Express to Edinburgh Waverley station. The trip takes about nine-and-a-half hours, including a wait at Manchester Piccadilly station.

Moules-frites (mussels and hot chips), an iron-rich dish.

The glorious Stade de France remains one of sport's great cathedrals. This is pre-match in 2013.

My partner Marcelle Gordon, Owen Nkumane and I at Stade de France for the host's make-or-break Soccer World Cup qualifying match against Ukraine in 2013. Les Blues got their much-needed 3-0 win to go through.

You don't often get treated to a home-cooked meal while on tour, but this was quite a feast in friend Damian Dussault's parental home in France in 2013.

Cassoulet, a dish from southern France, is a casserole with bountiful amounts of pork sausage and goose or duck – and some even add pork belly. It's a delight that has become one of our winter go-to dishes.

Hostellerie Bérard in the hilltop town of La Cadière d'Azur has a Michelin-star restaurant. After a tour in 2013, we were treated there one evening. This chicken confit is the best I've ever had.

By the time this trolley with a squeaking loose wheel stopped next to us at Hostellerie Bérard, we could eat no more. It had 38 different cheeses on it and, somehow, we found a gap.

East of Marseille is the small coastal town of Bandol. Its limestone hills make it a particularly productive wine region, and although I don't generally quaff rosé, I thought theirs was quite agreeable.

The humble croque monsieur is much more than a ham and cheese sandwich. I got hooked on the hard-baked crust of Emmental that unlocked the gooey generously layered inside.

Primarily made of offal, this dish proved a real delight in a wonderfully charming little restaurant oddly named The Box, in Padua, Italy in 2017. At first, some of my travel companions turned up their noses, but after tasting it, they couldn't "mmm" enough.

One of the chores of the job is watching practice. But we are only tolerated for the first 15 minutes.

On my way to Japan for the 2019 Rugby World Cup.

Tokyo from the hotel where the Springboks stayed. You can see why this megalopolis has 39 million inhabitants.

The Springboks and the All Blacks line up in Yokohama on the second day of the 2019 Rugby World Cup.

Fushimi Inari Shrine in Kyoto.

We found a wonderful Nepalese curry house in Omaezaki, a sleepy Japanese town. The South Africans literally took over the place for a week during the 2019 Rugby World Cup.

JJ Fredericks, the team logistics manager, and the Boks in Omaezaki in 2019.

Geishas at the Fushimi Inari Shrine.

I found the best chicken wings I've ever had in a Nagoya yakitori joint.

I had Kobe beef in Sydney once. During the 2019 Rugby World Cup, I got it at source, in Kobe in Japan.

his interrogator with sarcasm. He had a sense of haughtiness about him but it was actually quite endearing. Steve Hansen, the man who succeeded him, is the same but the former policeman just ends up sounding sardonic.

Jake White, another former schoolteacher, was fond of starting a sentence with "Again, like I said ..." when he knew he was set to repeat what he had just said three minutes earlier, or at a press conference three months previously. He said that once at a press conference in Ireland when a South African journo's phone rang. The lyrics to the start of the offending ring tone went: "Tennisballe, krieketballe, sokkerballe as jy wil" (Tennis balls, cricket balls, soccer balls if you have to). This was the opening refrain of a hideous but wildly popular Afrikaans song at the time titled "Leeuloop".

White held the traditions of the game and the Springboks dear, and would often talk about them. He obsessed, in a good way, about team selection. "In the past players were dropped and then you start again. I'm not going to do that. I've got to teach the players that I've got to get it right," he rather presciently told us in Perth in 2004. He won the RWC three years later.

Another former Bok coach, Rudolf Straeuli, when he believed he was required to respond to something that to him is clear and obvious, would start by saying: "Basically ..."

When he was Bok coach, Straeuli gave you the impression that he got some of his media training from the Stasi, but as turnarounds go, his has been remarkable. In fact, he just about rehabilitated, if not reinvented, himself first as commercial manager at the Sharks before joining the Lions where he started as chief executive officer.

Former Springbok assistant coach Gert Smal, like Straeuli,

often dead batted questions. With the taciturn Smal, though, you got the feeling his motives were not to suppress, but that sitting in front of a bank of cameras with bright lights and recorders simply did not appeal to him.

It was always advisable to catch Big Gert away from the top table where a question about the ruck, lineout, maul or scrum would be met far more favourably. It was only then that he would develop what looked suspiciously like a glint in his eye. I once asked him about the timing of the "hit" in the scrum engage and he appeared to spring to life.

Smal may have come across as placid and almost slothish in his demeanour, but don't be fooled. A colleague once referred to him and Allister Coetzee as White's "yes men" when they were Springbok assistant coaches. Coetzee was livid. Smal apparently wore the gaze of a man with homicidal intent when he finally got to confront the writer in question.

Heyneke Meyer almost permanently wore a steely gaze, but it was his mispronunciations that softened us up. For instance, for some reason no one ever corrected him when he spoke of South America's second-largest country "Argentinia".

Peter de Villiers had a go-to phrase when asked how he was doing. "Ag, you know, even the bad times are good," he'd say in clear reference to the 1967 Tremeloes hit. I often thought that he should have spent more time listening to that other Tremeloes ditty "Silence is Golden".

These quips and quirks served to liven up press conferences where one cliché tends to seamlessly follow the other. It of course doesn't help when Springbok media managers are just downright obstructionist. All too often writers are left with the suspicion that they see press conferences as a massive inconvenience. They know their existence is complicated when press conferences drift off script, and often players who are only likely to play a peripheral role in the next match or, worse, have been left holding tackle bags on tour, are presented for interviews.

Journalists who write for weekend papers despair because they are more likely to be affected by Springbok media managers' whims. Requests for interviews intended for weekend publication are generally made early in the week but often they don't materialise as envisioned. Interviews are either not arranged because the media manager couldn't bother, the subject or coach refuses, or the player is brought out as part of the team announcement, which means all the other hungry hounds get to shove their grubby recorders in front of him too.

To be fair, media managers simply don't have the clout they ought to have. If a player who has played more than 50 Tests isn't in the mood to do an interview, he can easily tell the team's media man to get lost. Often, though, writers are left with the sense that it's the inaction on the media manager's part, rather than the players refusing to be interviewed, that results in no-shows.

And it isn't just the South African media that suffer. Early in the week ahead of a Tri-Nations Test in Wellington in 2010, the local paper, the *Dominion Post*, requested an interview with Victor Matfield. The lock was closing in on 100 Tests later in the competition and the Kiwis have a deep appreciation for milestones even if it is someone they believe are one of the All Blacks' greatest adversaries. The paper simply wanted to put the elongated lock's name up in lights in their weekend edition.

Alas, Springbok media liaison Anthony Mackaiser didn't

follow through with the request and the paper didn't take kindly in their weekly gossip column. "We wish the Bok media manager was on the same flight home as Bakkies Botha [who was injured] because he has been as useful as a chocolate teapot. He should change his name to media prevention officer."

Jones jets in fuming

Eddie Jones had a reputation. Not only could he deliver a well-orchestrated press conference in the week leading up to a Test, but he would masterfully pull the strings like a puppeteer aimed at the mental degradation of his opponents.

He had quotable quotes at his fingertips.

"History is for coaches – players live in the present," he insisted on the eve of the RWC final in 2003 after being asked if his Wallabies team could repeat the heroics of their countrymen 12 years earlier. The Wallabies had just upset New Zealand to reach the final on home soil, and Jones was grinning from ear to ear.

The day before the final against England he reached for hyperbole. "When you talk about no tomorrows, this really is no tomorrow," said Jones.

Years later, as England coach Jones, albeit while addressing a corporate audience, said, "We've played 23 Tests and we've only lost one Test to the scummy Irish. I'm still dirty about that game but we'll get that back, don't worry." Jones later apologised for the remark.

"Arrogance is only bad when you lose," he reckoned on another occasion. "When you are winning and you are arrogant, then it is self-belief."

Whether he coaches Australia, Japan or England, Jones has standards. When he was coach of Japan he tore into his players after they lost to the French Barbarians in 2012. "It was a really poor performance," Jones was quoted in the *Japan Times*. "We showed no fight.

"We were completely outplayed at the set piece and I was disappointed with the players' attitude. They probably showed they don't want to play for Japan. At halftime I had to scream at them like a schoolteacher. The players don't want to win enough.

"We can't train any harder. We can't train with any more intent. The players understand the game plan but they weren't physical. How can you play rugby and not be physical? So we'll have to find players who can be physical. We've got a real problem in Japanese rugby. Our players aren't strong enough, they are not fit enough. They don't have the right attitude."

Often there is no real controversy but Jones would plot and stir and before you know it there's an obliging headline to suit his cause. Yet he's always ready with a smile and a quip, and an arching eyebrow that puts Roger Moore's to shame.

There's hardly a dull moment in a Jones press conference, so it was a little odd seeing the then Wallaby coach and his trusty lieutenant George Gregan walk into a meeting room at the erstwhile Louis Botha Airport in Durban with thunder writ over their faces.

They sat down in their grey suits and the manner in which they answered questions matched their facial expressions, limited largely to one-line answers, which was rather odd for the often garrulous Jones. Something was up but the assembled media didn't know what had raised the Aussies' ire. It was early in the week and the Wallabies had just flown in from Sydney via Joburg so it was unlikely something had happened here to piss the two off.

Eventually a Kiwi-born radio reporter seated to my immediate left asked Jones about a report in the Australian media the previous week in which the Wallaby camp seemed to suggest the Springboks' soft underbelly was in fact their pack of forwards. It is almost unthinkable – not just for the fact that the Boks' forward pack was one of their time-honoured strengths, but the Wallabies' forwards hardly ever bashed their opposite numbers into submission.

Jones sprung to life like a bunny with a new Duracell in his back. His left eyebrow arched as he turned his head from his interrogator to his diagonal left, to the right of the room where considerably fewer reporters sat.

"Why don't you direct that question to Mr Greenaway over there?" said Jones, pointing to the reporter now firmly in everyone's gaze.

After an awkward silence the seasoned hack said: "Uh, Eddie. That wasn't my story. I simply got the quotes from a report already written."

Now Jones's eyebrow arched like the Sydney Harbour Bridge. "What do you mean it wasn't your story?" Jones delved deeper.

"Well, it was from an existing report and I simply used the quotes. The report didn't originate with me."

"Well, where did it originate?" Jones demanded.

"I got it off a website."

"Which website?" the verbal ping-pong continued.

"I can't remember but I definitely got it off a website."

Jones was always up for a dramatic climax and this made

for a devilish denouement. "Now that wasn't a very good website now, was it, Mr Greenaway?"

Axe the captain

From the moment Paddy O'Brien sounded the final whistle at Twickenham on 23 November 2002, the Springboks had a date with destiny. England had just annihilated them 53–3 and South Africa's coach Rudolf Straeuli displayed what can only be described as back-to-the-wall belligerence.

He reminded the assembled media that the next time the teams were supposed to meet it would be in Perth the following year in a RWC pool match. "See you in Perth," was Straeuli's parting shot to local scribes who duly took that message and spread it across Her Majesty's semi-frozen island.

Fact is, Straeuli was clutching at straws. Not only did his team lose by a record margin to England that day, but they came up short against France 30–6 in Marseille and Scotland 21–6 at Murrayfield. Those defeats too came by record-losing margins for the Boks who, in mitigation, were beset by injuries that year.

Still, the coach was of the firm belief that if he could assemble the right personnel, hand them an uncluttered but effective blueprint and instil in them some belief, the Boks may yet have a chance at the RWC. In trying to achieve that objective, though, he had a few misadventures, including the notorious Kamp Staaldraad and a muddled selection policy. There was also a flare-up with distinct racial undertones between locks Quinton Davids and Geo Cronjé during a training camp. By the time the Boks arrived in Perth they had tumbled in global estimation, their meeting with England the one that left most of their supporters with fret.

The Boks opened their campaign with a resounding 72–6 win over Uruguay but their critics noted they should have been far more clinical. Oddly enough, O'Brien was the man in the middle.

England got their ball rolling with an 84–6 demolition of Georgia, setting the two heavyweights up for battle. But while the Boks and England set about their preparations, Georgia's players gave themselves a helluva time. They went sightseeing and absorbed as much as they could of Australia. When some of the travelling media bumped into them for the umpteenth time in Perth, one of the Georgians summed up their intrepidness. "When do you think we, from Georgia, are going to have the opportunity to see this again?" Fair enough.

By contrast, Straeuli's team seemed to have formed a laager. They felt under siege and by now they were heavyweights only in a historical sense. Despite a promising start in mid-2002, they had plodded along under Straeuli's guiding hand and were effectively here for a shot of redemption.

The problem is England had the experience, the bullet-proof game plan, the ball-winning pack, a management team setting trends. They also had an established match winner in Jonny Wilkinson, so they were bestowed the favourites tag, not just for this match but potentially the tournament.

The Boks lost 25–6 in a match in which their feistiness was an act in futility, meaning that, as Pool C winners, England could take the high road into the quarterfinals while the Boks were condemned to a last-eight meeting against old foe New Zealand.

Straeuli was still in search of a magic formula. Whatever he did before the RWC hadn't done the trick, as was proved by the defeat to England, and now he had to find solutions on the hoof.

Could he potentially tweak his already unimaginative game plan, or were there gains to be made in selection? It was these ponderables that drove conversation as some travelling media pushed back pints in an Irish pub in Brisbane in the lead-up to the Boks' last pool match against Samoa.

Although Samoa were going to put the Springboks through a bone-rattling physical examination, we were already looking ahead at the quarterfinals and what Straeuli could potentially do to somehow unsettle the All Blacks, then still in jittery pursuit of their second RWC title.

Of course some of the potential solutions presented at our table were soaked in parochialism, while others were just a hopeful stab in the dark. In any event, none of what we said was going to make a difference. Straeuli may have brought along a personal assistant who was tasked with filing what was being written about the Boks, but he was never going to take it on board.

Some of our bar-room talk revolved around the somewhat treasonous notion of dropping tour captain Corné Krige for the wrecking-ball tyro Schalk Burger. Burger, some of us argued, would throw his then young body around like a man possessed and may yet have a bigger impact on the match. His presence would certainly be felt at the rucks where Richie McCaw was again likely to rule the roost for the All Blacks.

Besides, as one seasoned writer would often say about Krige's captaincy, "It was tainted by failure," which also taps into the narrative that the captain could have done more to prevent his players descending into a pit naked at Kamp Staaldraad.

Krige, of course, was a whole-hearted player who would run through brick walls for the cause and an engaging captain when it came to dealing with the media. He didn't deserve to be dropped and, in any event, this idea was a flight of fancy and no one was actually going to write it.

Some of us who were at the previous RWC remembered too well how tour captain Joost van der Westhuizen reacted to the assertion that his squad had been split in two. A weekend-newspaper article suggested during the pool stages of that RWC that Rassie Erasmus should perhaps take over the reins as he was more tactically astute than the revered 1995 RWC winner.

Back in Brisbane, we finished our pints – but not, incidentally, before two Afrikaans-daily writers were berated for trying to "share a round" when it came to payment, which is deeply frowned upon by touring journos. We were happy we had solved all the Springboks' problems, and usually that is where we'd leave it.

A day or so later, at the team announcement for the Samoa match, we had readied ourselves for a long interrogation of Straeuli. RWC team-announcement press conferences are a little different in that, apart from the coach and the captain, some players selected for the match must also avail themselves for interviews.

We were all seated when Straeuli walked in, followed by Krige, team manager Gideon Sam, and players including Victor Matfield, Joost van der Westhuizen and Joe van Niekerk.

Despite the pall that seemed to shroud the room from the moment they walked in, Van Niekerk, a man with a magnetic smile, grinned cheerily, even giving some reporters a wave. The overall mood, though, was tense. Straeuli, even more monotone than usual, started reading out the names of the players to do duty against Samoa. "Number 15 is Jaco van der Westhuyzen, right wing is Ashwin Willemse," and so on.

After Straeuli read out, "Number 5 lock is Victor Matfield, Number 6 flank and captain is Corné Krige," something strange happened. He paused. "And this is for Kevin McCallum sitting over there," he said, looking in the direction of the reporter. "The role of the fetcher flank is ..." continued the coach laying bare the duties and responsibilities of the No. 6 in South African terms.

Clearly, the reporter in question had turned our bar talk into a look-ahead article to the team announcement and the coach and the captain were far from impressed. McCallum had to do a live crossing for a Joburg-based radio station and did not stay for the end of the press conference. Krige apparently later went after him, but in vain.

"Fatalistic incomprehension"

The Boks had been on a five-match winning streak in 2008 but would that winning run continue under new coach Peter de Villiers on their end-of-year tour?

That week in the build-up to their Test against England would be the first time the English press would be exposed to De Villiers's quirks and often incongruent ramblings. The press arrived and milled around outside a function room below decks at the splendid Royal Garden Hotel in Kensington, London. But the press conference that followed was, let's say, a little bizarre. Some of the British hacks would turn to their South African colleagues with a look of utter bemusement during proceedings.

The UK's *Independent* perhaps best captured the mood at De Villiers's team announcement ahead of the Test.

"An audience with Peter de Villiers is not what one would term 'a predictable experience'. Indeed, for the uninitiated there is the danger of being bamboozled to the point of inertia," wrote their reporter. "Asked if he was tired after a tumultuous year, he said: 'What me? No, no, no. This is a great city and I don't want to be fatigued looking around at all your great heritage. No, no, no, there's no time to be fatigued. You get one life, you must live it to the full. It's going to be your own fault, young man, if you miss something great in life.'

"Later he offered: 'There are South Africans playing well everywhere over here. It goes on and on. South Africans are taking over England and that's a worrying factor for the Englishman.'

"Asked about the channel between England's outside-half and inside-centre that Australia exploited last week, 'It won't be bad this Saturday,' he assured us. 'We know [Riki] Flutey as we played against him a lot in the Super 14. And we all know Capriati is not a bad player.' Yes, we do, but we also can tell Danny apart from Jennifer," the scribe reported.

The paper damningly noted that "it all soon descended into fatalistic incomprehension".

By then De Villiers hadn't just developed the habit of mixing his metaphors, his thoughts were simply muddled.

"You know you don't have any control over winning and losing, but you can control how you play the game," he said, and to be fair, that kind of claptrap wasn't unique to him – some of his countrymen, who draw inspiration from above, often offered that disclaimer when it suited them.

"I'm a man in my own right," the coach famously said. "If they appointed me for rugby coaching they appointed the right person. When I walk away from this job I want to say one thing: 'I did it my way.'"

The British and Irish Lions tour of 2009 presented the Brits with another taste of De Villiers shooting off his mouth when he enthusiastically sprung to the defence of Schalk Burger, banned for eight weeks for eye gouging Luke Fitzgerald during that tour.

"We have brilliant players in this country, most of them world class," said the coach. "We do not prepare them to do things you would see in the bushveld. If you want to eye-gouge a Lion, that is where you go," said the coach.

Clearly, his comments embarrassed his employers and De Villiers was forced into an apology days later.

Often he would verbally joust with journalists. Early in his tenure a woman reporter was incensed by the scornful way in which he spoke to her after a press conference. "Young lady, let me tell you something ..." he started his diatribe about rugby in the Struggle days. She set the record straight, laying bare to the ill-informed coach her family's struggles in the Struggle.

But she wasn't the only one the coach rubbed up the wrong way in that press conference. Perhaps tired of hearing questions from the rotund Ken Borland, De Villiers referred to the writer as "die kortste mannetjie met die langste vrae" (the shortest little man with the longest questions).

Borland took it in his, albeit short, stride, but some of us were aghast. But what De Villiers said then pales in comparison with his actions after his last Test in charge of the Springboks two years later.

The Boks had just lost a tense, nerve-jangling RWC quarterfinal to Australia 11–9 in Wellington and the coach, whose contract was not going to be renewed, wanted to have the last say. His parting shot to the media was one you sense he had sat on for a while.

As a couple of writers walked out of the Westpac Stadium past the Springbok team bus, De Villiers, who was already on board, took the time to get up and left them with: "The best thing about leaving this job is not having to see you fuckers again."

One writer had to be restrained.

The Harry moment

Almost exactly a decade earlier, Harry Viljoen, one of De Villiers's predecessors, also said his goodbyes in an inglorious blaze.

Viljoen's team had struggled on their end-of-year tour to France, Italy and England before they played the United States in Houston. They had lost to France in Paris and even more convincingly to England in London and the end of a long season was in sight. The Test was set to be played on 1 December, which is unusual because it is rare that the Boks drag their on-field commitments into the last month of the year. This also meant that once they boarded their flight to Houston, hair – or should that be Harry? – was always going to be let down with all manner of off-the-field shenanigans. So by the time Viljoen's team unconvincingly beat the Eagles 43–20 at one of the local colleges the coach was done having to explain himself to the media.

"I hope there are no more questions. I'm going home for Christmas and I really don't want to speak to you lot again," said the coach who famously negotiated his contract with SA Rugby from his yacht in the Mediterranean.

It proved a self-fulfilling prophecy because a month or so later he quit somewhat unexpectedly.

Fast Eddie

Following the Wallabies' shock win over the All Blacks in the semifinal of the 2003 RWC, things went a little off script when Eddie Jones had to address the media.

First, the microphone operated sporadically, which as you can imagine, given the moment, was a greater source of frustration for the coach than the media. When it did finally work, a "reporter" in a Wallabies jersey stood up.

"First, guys," he said, "congratulations. Thanks for winning because I went out and bought this fricken jumper and it would have looked really bad had you lost."

He then got to his question: "Now, uh, this week, what made it a little different? Did George [Gregan] have an extra bit of Weet-Bix? Did you let them train harder? Did you watch more videos? Explain to the average bloke in the street, because we have no idea."

The Wallabies, you see, were under huge pressure to win the RWC on home soil. They had won the second instalment of the competition in 1991 under captain Nick Farr-Jones in the United Kingdom and repeated that success more or less on the same soil under John Eales in 1999.

Four years on, the expectation was great for Jones and Gregan to deliver the trophy on home soil. It was often remarked that a Wallaby win on home soil would have helped popularise the sport, which was continuing to struggle for participating numbers behind Aussie Rules, Rugby League and cricket.

What further moved the reporter to ask what he did was Jones's calculated decision to base his team in Coffs Harbour for much of the tournament. The beach town is about 550 kilometres north of Sydney and it was to provide Jones and his squad the kind of privacy to deal with the job at hand. That relative isolation, however, meant that reporters like the one standing in the Wallaby jersey didn't have a fricken clue what was going on.

"That's a fair dinkum question, is it?" Jones asked in mild astonishment. "Nice jumper you've got, but maybe you need a smaller size.

"There was a lot of attention to detail in our preparation this week and maybe there was a bit more sugar on the WeetBix," continued Jones.

Not long after there was a question – uh, make that statement – from the floor.

"Mr Jones, you are really harshly criticised by the media here, especially by the people sitting in front of you today. Very harshly, viciously at times. Do you feel vindicated?" asked what we assumed was a news reporter.

"It's the media's job to pass comment. I don't have any problem with that," said Jones, but not before said reporter had positioned himself towards the middle of the room to snap a picture of the coach.

"Phil [Waugh], your haircut's looking really good," came another observation from the floor.

"Thanks, mate," Waugh replied sheepishly.

Jones, however, was a little irked when asked about the areas in which he believed the Wallabies beat the All Blacks. According to the coach, he had answered that question after Australia's 50–21 defeat to the All Blacks earlier that year in the Tri-Nations.

"I'm not going to tell you, mate," said the coach. "We are going to play New Zealand again. I remember saying it at a press conference, and you people laughed at me. You can enjoy your laughter again," said the tetchy coach.

Jones was a little more relaxed when asked whom he would prefer to play in the final. England were scheduled to meet France the following day.

"I would like to see Jason Leonard drop kicking with Raphael Ibanez at the end around about midnight. Whoever kicks the last kick we'll be happy to play."

Melbourne meltdown

The laboured way Rudolf Straeuli walked into the press room in the bowels of the Telstra Dome in 2003 could not have been more different to Nick Mallett's swagger at the same stage four years earlier.

Mallett's team, you see, had just beaten one of the tournament favourites in the quarterfinals and the smile almost wrapped around the coach's head. He had in tow his captain Joost van der Westhuizen and Jannie de Beer. His team had just triumphed, slightly against the odds, against Clive Woodward's burgeoning England team, toppling their chariot just when it seemed it was building a head of steam.

De Beer, of course, had been hugely instrumental, landing five drop goals in one of the Springboks' most famous triumphs post isolation. Although one of his comments were perhaps deliberately taken out of context, De Beer's "The Lord gave me the talent, the forwards gave me the ball" remains one of the most enduring Springbok post-match one-liners.

Four years on, Straeuli would have been justified asking for some divine intervention. His team had just been unceremoniously dumped from the tournament by New Zealand and now the hounds were about to be set loose on Straeuli.

His win record stood at a paltry 52 per cent but that was almost the least of Straeuli's concerns. It wasn't just the low win rate that made him the South African public's sporting enemy number one. There was a row with distinct racial undertones between the locks in his preliminary squad, Geo Cronjé and Quinton Davids, not to mention how by then the naked truth was emerging back home of his infamous pre-tournament boot camp, Kamp Staaldraad.

Straeuli would have been aware of the storm back home. For heaven's sake, he knew everything we wrote on that tour as he brought his PA along specifically for that task.

Straeuli is one of the most undemonstrative coaches you are likely to meet. He was typically calm. He was in that seat to talk about his team's defeat to the All Blacks and possibly the road forward, not what was unfolding back home.

"We came here to win the World Cup and we didn't," he said in his monotone baritone. "We won a lot of hearts for the way we played at this tournament but maybe the World Cup did come a year too soon."

I remember questioning in my report whose hearts the Boks might have captured in their tryless exploits when it mattered most against England and then New Zealand.

SA Rugby's managing director Rian Oberholzer was also of the view that the RWC had arrived 12 months too soon. "If we had another year, especially when you consider the success of the under-21 team, who knows what would have happened?

"We hope the young players will have learnt from this experience so that we can apply it and we can be proud of the Springbok team. We can't be proud of the team if different forces are trying to pull the team apart.

"I would like to see the core of the guys who played in this tournament be back in 2007," said Oberholzer.

He was partly granted that wish. Bakkies Botha, Schalk Burger, Jaque Fourie, Victor Matfield, Danie Rossouw, John Smit, Juan Smith, Jean de Villiers and Ashwin Willemse were all selected for Jake White's squad that lifted the Webb Ellis Cup four years later. Fourie, Rossouw, Smith, Burger, Matfield, Botha and Smit played in the final.

As the press conference unfolded, Oberholzer stood to the side, well away from the cameras. But, with Straeuli's interrogation done, South African reporters turned their recorders to him. He was defiant. He backed the coach.

"I don't know why that question is posed so often and I don't want to sound aggressive, but the coach was appointed until 2005 and part of that term is this World Cup," he said after being asked about Straeuli's future.

Oberholzer was either oblivious or just blind to the fallout back home. Besides, the writers on tour all had sports and news editors wanting to know why Straeuli and indeed Oberholzer weren't falling on their sword.

"He wasn't appointed to win the World Cup but to coach

the Springbok team," continued Oberholzer. "Obviously we are disappointed we didn't go any further in the World Cup. We had a difficult draw. Circumstances outside the control of the team played a role but I think they did very well."

It was about at that moment I checked to see if my device was still recording and whether indeed I was awake. Did Oberholzer actually just say that?

"We have a fantastic young team and we have to try and keep them together. Continuity is important to us. We should keep our cool and move forward," he said. He did concede, though, that the Boks fell short of the minimum requirement set for them that they should reach the semifinals. For that to happen, however, they would have had to beat a top side like England or New Zealand, and that was always unlikely as the Boks under Straeuli could only beat one of the world's top sides in the two years he was in charge: Australia.

"That was always going to be a hard task," Oberholzer acknowledged. "We would have to beat numbers one and two in the world. We didn't set ourselves the easiest target."

A little later Oberholzer left and the mini media scrum dispersed. By the time a security guard pushed open a stadium exit leading to a bridge over the railway lines that separate the stadium from the city, Oberholzer was already about 30 metres or so in front in tight formation with his partner.

They looked happy, and for some reason I was happy for them.

Oberholzer, though, was about to cross a bridge in more ways than one. Less than a month later, the players turned on him and he quit.

Heyneke, it's all about the here (and now)

No one can accuse Heyneke Meyer of not being passionate about his job. His press-conference explanations often involved a fair amount of rambling, which meant the bulk of it failed to make it into print. But he would often avail himself for chats away from the microphones and cameras and that proved helpful in getting some insight into his psyche and thought processes.

His preoccupation with size did not endear him to many Springbok fans. "How could he let CJ Stander go?" or "What has Heinrich Brüssow done wrong?" fans often wondered.

Meyer fastidiously held on to the belief that a good big player will always be better than a good small one. Often enough, he articulated the sentiment: "Rugby is not a contact sport. It is a collision sport."

During the build-up to a 2014 Test in Perth in which Bryan Habana played his hundredth Test and in which he was sinbinned, I made a simple enquiry about ruck defence at the conclusion of a press conference.

The coach had opted to push into battle a back row that consisted of Francois Louw, Marcell Coetzee and Duane Vermeulen and their showdown with ball-poaching Michael Hooper and co. was going to be key to the outcome of the match. I was met by an unexpectedly detailed explanation that included a prop. No, not a front-row forward, but the team's media manager De Jongh Borchardt. The coach rather warmed to the opportunity of sharing his insights as he ordered Borchardt to the floor. With Borchardt prone in a sideways position on the deck, Meyer proceeded to demonstrate how the defending player should go about his business – a scene made even more bizarre because of the stack of media guide books that had to double as the ball.

Needless to say, a hotel staffer who passed through the door was rather perplexed when he walked in on this peculiar scene.

Eye on the prize

Sometimes coaches are so focused on trying to get their team in the best possible shape that they detach themselves from their surroundings. There is of course nothing wrong with being focused on the job at hand, but it can create the impression of a coach being one dimensional.

In the build-up to the Springboks' final end-of-year tour Test against France in Paris in 2013, Heyneke Meyer was hardly under pressure. In the preceding weeks his team beat Wales 24–15 in Cardiff (with Bismarck du Plessis, Willem Alberts and Duane Vermeulen making thumping tackles) and was ruthlessly efficient in beating Scotland 28–0 in Edinburgh (in a match in which fullback Willie le Roux touched the stars). Meyer was now going for the end-of-year tour clean sweep, desperate to become only the second Springbok coach (after Kitch Christie) since readmission to deliver two clean sweeps of Europe.

Besides, the Boks had not beaten France in Europe since Nick Mallett's marauding team conquered all in 1997. Meyer was keen to join the Christie club – who wouldn't be?

Meyer had his eye so firmly on Saturday's prize that he had thoroughly insulated himself from the mood – not just on the streets of Paris, but well beyond the capital. You see, the French national football team had just qualified for the following year's Soccer World Cup by overturning a three-goal advantage in the last qualifier against the Ukraine at the Stade de France, where the Boks were due to play.

I was at that match and there was no mistaking the French mood. People poured onto the Champs Élysées. For heaven's sake, surely we can remember how the 1995 RWC lifted the mood in this country?

That seemed to escape the Bok camp, however.

This is an extract from one of my reports for the outlets in the then Times Media filed two days before the Test:

"France are atop a wave of patriotic euphoria after their national team in their national sport avoided the guillotine by slipping through the back door to qualify for next year's football World Cup in Brazil.

"There must exist the chance of that Gallic fervour again spilling over at the majestic Stade de France when the Boks run out there on Saturday but Meyer's gaze is firmly fixed on his team's state of readiness. Some may call his view insular but it tallies with a great self belief that if the Boks do what they do well, external factors matter little.

"'I will tell you in all honesty that I was so focused on this game that I wasn't even aware of the game,' said the coach."

I was a little stunned that Meyer was unaware of the events that had unfolded around 40 hours earlier because he would have had to be in his room, curtains closed, with mobile and television off.

That blinkered view, however, seems to work for him because the Boks recorded their first ever win over France at the Stade de France that Saturday.

❖ ❖ ❖

Jake White was similarly detached from what was happening up the road on a Bok visit to Scotland in 2007.

White can be forgiven, though. He was applying the finishing touches to the Springboks' preparations for the 2007 RWC. The Boks beat Connacht 18–3 in Galway before crossing the Irish Sea for an appointment with Scotland at Murrayfield where they were unable to secure enough beds for their bulky squad in Edinburgh and had to set up camp in Peebles, around 36 kilometres south.

In the build-up to the game White was asked by the press why they were staying in Peebles and not Edinburgh. "We couldn't get enough hotel beds. I think there's a concert taking place." That "concert" happened to be the Edinburgh Festival.

What's up, Doc?

Jannie du Plessis's engaging manner often endeared him to scribes looking for something a little different in press conferences. He had a matter-of-fact way of telling it like it is, which was a refreshing departure from the almost sterilised way in which his teammates were coached into answering questions.

In one press conference in Edinburgh, Du Plessis proved an important ally to the Afrikaans press when it came to matters of the heart on an end-of-year tour in 2012. After team doctor Craig Roberts used terms such as "atrial fibrillation", "high-frequency waves" and "nerve cells" in explaining Tendai Mtawarira's rare heart condition, one writer was in the dark about how he should translate the terms. Roberts's Afrikaans is limited and was of no help. Du Plessis, who is also a medical doctor, came to the writer's aid. He sketched a rough diagram of a heart, showing the four chambers and the arteries, and then supplied the translation to the troublesome terms.

On a trip to the Antipodes, Du Plessis's engaging way left Kiwi reporters wide eyed after one of them asked how he spent his days practising as a doctor. By then some of the local hacks were keen to shift the focus from writing what they perceived to be a weakened Springbok squad Jake White had assembled for the away leg of the Tri-Nations in 2007.

Du Plessis certainly gave them the diversion they wanted. The tighthead told us about his days and nights working in the casualty ward in one of Bloemfontein's state hospitals. Like most doctors, he had a matter-of-fact manner of laying bare the facts. I always found him friendly and thoroughly engaging.

"It depends on what happens on the weekend," he told our media pod when asked how he'd spend a typical shift. "When Bloemfontein Celtic plays Kaizer Chiefs and they beat Kaizer Chiefs, we see stab wounds and drunk people.

"When they play rugby, we see car accidents. And then you get your usual stuff. There are a lot of chronic patients.

"Unbelievable, yeah.

"We see about 100 people in an eight-hour shift between two or three people. People get cross and use broken bottles [as weapons]. They usually go for the eyes. I have seen lots of people die.

"I talked to a guy, a specialist from England, who came to do some practical work. He puts in intercostal drains and it takes 15 years to learn to be that sort of surgeon.

"Seeing stab wounds every weekend, I have put in 20 drains in one night. So, I think practically being able to do stuff is a very good environment to be able to study and learn and hone your skills a bit.

"If you want to do trauma and emergency medicine, I don't think there's a better place on Earth. Maybe Central Africa, but there you don't have the stuff to do it. You want a place where you have the facilities to be able to do procedures."

I was aware of what Du Plessis does when armed with a stethoscope but the Kiwis looked at him wide eyed in astonishment.

In Jean's words

As mentioned, press conferences can be dreadful. Familiar faces answer familiar questions in a familiar style and before long you feel you know what the coach or captain is going to say before the interrogation even starts. This is especially true when a coach signs up from one RWC to the next because he is likely to want to install a captain who will walk that entire journey with him.

We had John Smit for eight years but, thankfully, he was articulate, thoughtful and wired right to meet the demands of a leader in his position in the New South Africa. He did it with aplomb.

When Smit moved on, Jean de Villiers was bestowed the honour by Meyer. Tradition, ethos and team culture are values De Villiers held dear but he wasn't a slave to them. He knew the gravity of his task, but accepted it with a laidback grace that immediately put those around him at ease. He soon warmed to the task of conducting the captain's press conference the day before the game, which is quite an achievement given how easily you can fall into the same verbal routine on the eve of a clash.

The Boks play 12 to 14 Tests a year, so if their captain remains fit he had better show some mental vitality too, or run the risk of being called boring. De Villiers, however, took it in his stride, which meant he was up for the odd left-field enquiry. In fact, he had become so settled that I cornered him with a strange request as he walked into the interview room one Friday morning.

I reminded him of the pitfalls of having to face the media alone every Friday before a match and put it to him that we should keep it interesting. De Villiers is a curious soul and immediately wanted to know more.

"Why don't I give you a 'mystery' word before the Friday presser and see if you can work it in in one of your answers?"

He paused for half a second before asking: "Okay, what's today's word?"

Not having given it much thought myself, I said something like "indiscriminate", I think.

The idea was to give him a word that kept him on his toes but didn't cause him to stumble. It meant that those of us who were in on it listened more intently than usual to the start of a sentence and its general construction to see whether the mystery word was about to follow. Even the media manager would demand to be given the word before the captain sat down in front of the microphones.

De Villiers proved a good sport for much of that season.

In one press conference we could hear him building up

to using, I think "tantalising", but suddenly interrupted himself. He stopped and then said: "I'm sorry, I'm just thinking of something else."

As it turned out, the media manager and I faced each other at opposite ends of the room and for obvious reasons we turned around to face the wall.

Tales from the pack

"Ja, no definitely," boomed Bakkies Botha in all his incongruent glory after rejoining the Springbok squad after a two-year absence. He had last played against Namibia in the 2011 RWC in North Harbour, but had now been roped in from Toulon to play against Scotland at Murrayfield.

"When I arrived the only South African there was Joe van Niekerk and since then they are coming in fast," said Botha about the South African proliferation in the south of France. "I don't know what pulls them, is it the euro or the boerewors? I love it when the guys phone me, even the Australian Matt Giteau. They ask, 'Can I fetch a packet of boerie?' I say, 'Come past, I'll give you one.'"

Of course the suggestiveness of it all was far too much for some.

The vastly experienced Wallaby lock Nathan Sharpe found himself in a pod of rugby scribes hungry to find out more about a loose forward who was set to make his 2010 Test debut against the Boks in Brisbane.

"I always laugh when the Western Force are talking about signing him. The coaching staff used the phrase 'He's got some shit about him,'" said Sharpe, which naturally drew some bemused reactions.

"I don't know what that means but I think it is something good," said Sharpe.

As in any marriage, even some of the most enduring partnerships can face testing times as John Smit and Victor Matfield discovered on one Tri-Nations trip to New Zealand in 2010.

Smit, you see, struggled to find Matfield, the Boks' principle lineout jumper in a defeat to the All Blacks in Auckland. Facing up to the press later, Smit said: "He gave me the look my wife gives me when I come home late."

Matfield later explained the gravity of Smit's sins: "We've got a good relationship and he knows how I feel about the lineout."

The then rookie lock Pieter-Steph du Toit gushed about meeting Bakkies Botha for the first time on an end-of-year tour in 2013.

"I only met Bakkies last night and I'm really excited about working with him. He's been a very nice person so far," Du Toit told us in Cardiff.

One journo was quick to point out to Du Toit that the sometimes miscreant Botha would be happy to share helpful information like "what not to do in disciplinary hearings".

Seven

Being Black

This chapter deals primarily with being a black media practitioner while travelling abroad with the Springboks.

Sometimes you encounter racism, but mostly you are just the victim of being a peculiarity in someone else's eyes. Late night in Buenos Aires you may be asked, "Where are the drugs?" Airport security might ask you to step aside more than they do your travel companions. Japanese kids may look at you, fascinated to the core, as if you've just stepped out of their video game. More often than not, you are able to laugh it off.

Shifting tides

THANKFULLY – SLOWLY, AND at times imperceptibly – attitudes have changed and you are less the outcast than you were, say, 20 years ago. Maybe that's because there are more black writers, but even back in the mid-1990s there were slightly more dark-skinned scribes than actual black Springboks.

Back then, and for years after, the racism hit you in the face because, well, South Africa is supposed to be home.

These are perhaps not typical examples but they serve to illustrate how we as black writers have had to just suck it up.

You may, for instance, find yourself walking with a fellow black rugby writer to a Test match at Loftus Versfeld when you quickly have to assess how you are going to deal with the racists who have decided to insert themselves into your day. Having parked at Pretoria Girls' High, we have to run the gauntlet to pass several burly men socialising next to their gas braais and bakkies. There's the whiff of boerewors, "wiff" some onions.

We have our laptop bags dangling over our shoulders and our accreditation lanyards around our necks. The brandy-guzzling louts size us up from a distance but become less boisterous the nearer we get. I more or less know what's next, but my younger colleague hasn't walked these dusty streets before.

Just as we pass them – in other words, we don't get the opportunity to see the perpetrator – one of them chirps after clearing his throat: "Uh, die sokker is môre, nê." (The football is tomorrow, hey.)

I have to gently tug my colleague's arm to ensure our continued safe passage to the gates of Loftus.

A few years later, as luck would have it, the same colleague and I are walking from a Test match at Kings Park. We have to make our way to one of the outer fields because that's where SA Rugby deemed fit for us to park. By then the final whistle had long gone and we had attended both press conferences and filed copy so the spectators walking back to their vehicles at that hour are likely to have had a few dops.

A beggar comes up to a man in a Springbok jersey. As he waves the beggar away he spots us. "You must help your people," he slurs at my colleague who this time requires more than a gentle tug to ensure our safe passage to our rental vehicle.

Thankfully, often what we experience abroad for being black is more worthy of a chuckle.

Darkness falls over the Andes

Friday before match day is frantic. Previews need to be written, the Springbok captain's sentiments need to be neatly captured in his customary pre-match press conference and there are usually features to finish.

It's no different as Jean de Villiers delivers his pre-match sermon at the team's appropriately named Diplomatic Hotel in Mendoza. For once we can't wait for him to finish. Some of us have already written our features for the weekend editions and have practically already written our previews and are now just blending De Villiers's comments with what we've already written.

The reason for our indecent haste is the half-day trip we've booked into the Andes. If we can get our work done by midday it would be worth the effort, so we beaver away at our keyboards and soon set off to the tour operator's office.

We drive out of Mendoza and head for the imposing mountain range to the west. Mendoza, located in the Andes foothills, is only 365 kilometres from the Chilean capital Santiago. That sounds simple enough, but it is over extreme mountainous terrain, and you have to factor in traffic and a potential six-hour wait just to cross the border. Thankfully, our plans don't include crossing the border. We want to see as much as we can on this side of the great mountain range.

Our tour guide informs us that we will also head for a derelict hotel, which has become a tourist attraction. The hotel – well, resort actually – was built by the government in the 1930s with the purpose of providing an escape for high-ranking officials. Argentina is big and there's plenty of room to escape into its nooks and crannies.

As our small bus pulls up, another larger one is trying to park without being a hazard. The complex is nestled on the edge of a mountain and you can tell the place has history and, at some point, had prestige.

We head up some steps and a few of the occupants of the other bus catch up. High-school kids, some of whom are a little giddy. At the top, instead of turning right towards what appears to be the hotel, we head straight into a small chapel that has its doors wide open. Colleague Vata Ngobeni and I head in. We have barely looked around when Tintin, one of our colleagues and travel companions, rather nervously summons us outside. "Guys, guys … Guys, you need to come here," he says, waving us closer.

Vata and I head back out. Tintin is standing with six or so of the high-school girls but the others are also taking an interest. He explains that they want to take pictures with Vata and me. It seems a bit odd, but Vata and I oblige and we're soon flanked by two long-haired Argentinean girls. No sooner is that moment captured when two more smiling faces head our way with the same request. Again we oblige, and then two more follow, and so on. Now it's starting to feel awkward.

There must be between 30 and 40 of them. This seems ridiculous. We aren't sure whether we're being mistaken for famous musicians or actors. Eventually, we call it to a halt and suggest that perhaps it is best for us just to take one large group picture. Some faces drop, but soon we are in one large formation and our tour guide steps several metres back to start taking group shots with different cameras now strewn in front of him.

It looks and feels bizarre, but this is Argentina. As we head to the nearby restaurant I ask the tour guide what that was all about. He chuckles before informing us that, given their accents, the girls are probably from Corrientes in northern Argentina and that this is more than likely the first time they've seen black men in the flesh.

Going bananas

Tournament afterparties are sometimes the stuff of legend. The Hong Kong Sevens doesn't disappoint. All the participating teams descend on a function room in the Furama Hotel and the place goes off. There is a commitment to getting hammered that I've never seen before.

On my way to the gents I almost walk into the puddle Wales flyhalf Neil Jenkins had deposited on the floor. To be fair, Jenkins doesn't even know where he is. He is seated, by then alone, with his head resting on his left hand. His eyes are shut and it's entirely possible that when he opens them again it may be to add to what he has already left on the floor.

In the gents I'm introduced to one of the Hong Kong team's locks. I forget his name but he is introduced as "The Gorilla" and I can immediately tell why. He has a forehead that goes on for days.

I'm informed that the afterparty will be at a place called

Joe Bananas, which is apparently a must-stop for anyone who attends the Sevens. With such a reputation, I am rather looking forward to pulling into Joe Bananas but my enthusiasm is doused when my taxi grinds to a halt outside the establishment.

I have an aversion to queues and this is a long one. But I have to see what all the fuss is about so I join the back. Clearly, the place is pumping but there also seems to be a commotion. One of the two bouncers keeps opening the door to peek in. He looks increasingly alarmed when he briefs his colleague. Now there are sounds other than that of music emanating from the establishment.

There are bangs, the odd thud, the sound of breaking glass, and of course women screaming. The noise intensifies and it is clear that there's a fight in progress. It sounds so hectic that some of the folk ahead of me in the queue drift off to seek a quieter establishment.

The doormen now look a little panicked. One of them takes another peek inside and now the fight seems to be happening just on the other side of the door so they yank open the door and storm in. The scene that unfolds isn't exactly what I've been expecting. Given the noise, and the duration of this conflict, I had figured two teams must be smashing up the place.

What is in fact transpiring is the eviction of one of Papua New Guinea's players, and he isn't leaving quietly. The structural integrity of his dark trousers is intact but his shirt had been ripped to shreds. Scratch and cut marks are visible on his chest, with spots of blood making for a striking contrast on his once-white shirt.

Eight, if not 10, bouncers have been deployed for this

task and still they struggle to subdue the belligerent brawler. Players from Papua New Guinea can be quite bellicose on the field and I'm mildly surprised that his teammates aren't part of the action.

Eventually the bouncers drag him outside, but he is still kicking and swinging. By now the local constabulary has arrived, but they dutifully prefer to wait for the staff to effect the eviction and only once he is prone on the ground do they step forward and cuff him.

He is finally dragged off but that would be the bloodiest bar eviction I have ever witnessed until an obstinate and bellicose drunk in equal measure is removed from the premises of a bar called Sam's in Cardiff in November 2000. There, it was left to one bouncer, who looked vastly experienced, to remove the strapping fella with pure pugilistic intent. It dragged on for a while – to the soundtrack of Ricky Martin's "She Bangs", Anastasia's "Out of Love", the then J.Lo's "Let's get Loud" and perhaps appropriately 'N Sync's "Bye Bye" – before the troublemaker is involuntarily but inexorably ushered to the exit.

The sound that made the biggest impact, however, was that of the bloke bouncing off the walls and the wooden stairway that leads to a side exit on St Mary's Street. I digress.

Back in Hong Kong, the bouncers pull themselves together and then point some of us to the door. I'm in. The signs of fight are everywhere but the party is still very much in swing. I grab a beer, which sets me back the equivalent of roughly R36. I can't get pissed here, I tell myself.

At some point, I meet a dreadlocked bloke from Jamaica named Colin, I think. We hit it off, but later we drift off to different conversations. When I spot him again he's chatting to an attractive blonde who has held on to her looks. He introduces me, and our time in Joe Bananas is just getting better. We're getting a few curious looks, however – at least Colin is.

Then a young man, probably in his early twenties, detaches himself from the group he's in and starts talking to the blonde. He doesn't seem happy. The music is too loud so we don't know what his beef is, but whatever she tells him makes him turn on his heels.

Colin asks her what that was all about. She tells us that that was her son and he isn't happy seeing his mom on the dance floor with a black guy. Colin and I look at each other.

She's mildly embarrassed and we stop short of laughing. But suddenly there's shouting, and the sound is coming our way. Her son is heading back but it doesn't look like he's the problem. He's trying to hold onto the arm of a younger bloke who has fire in his eyes. His younger brother.

The two confront us. Well, I'm not sure who exactly. The younger one loses it and goes for Colin while his mother tries to berate him. Just as a proper scuffle is about to ensue the bouncers, now well rested from their earlier exertions, step in.

They separate Colin and Fury Boy. They are not interested in an inquest and invite Colin and me to the door. Now the blonde berates them too but they ignore her.

Colin and I shake our heads knowingly. We were always going to be the guys asked to leave and as we sit on the pavement watching another sunrise in Hong Kong we remind ourselves, that's just how the world turns.

Beige suede shoes blues

Commentator Owen Nkumane and I are in a queue. It's a long one, but we can tell from the outside why folk have flocked to the establishment. It's late afternoon, early evening and Brisbane is loin-drippingly steamy.

Eventually we're at the front of the queue. One of the Samoan-looking bouncers turns to us, and enquires, "How are you boyz?" His colleague gives us the once over with his eyes. Down, then up.

"Can't let you in," he says out of the blue. I think we more than meet the establishment's smart-casual sartorial requirement. He runs the rule over Owen again. "It's him," he says pointing.

"What's wrong with him?" I demand to know.

"It's those shoes," the bouncer offers teasingly.

"What's wrong with his shoes?" I continue my search for answers.

"They're not funky, clubby enough," the bouncer says with a straight face.

By now I suspect they're just taking the mickey, but they aren't.

Owen is looking down at his spotless beige suede shoes. "They're Timberlands, man. Timberlands," he remonstrates.

The bouncer shakes his head before stretching out his left arm to indicate we should leave the queue. We do so reluctantly. Besides, he'd probably throw me as far as a javelin.

We don't move off, however. We know we've just been bounced from a queue for no good reason and we are not leaving quietly.

"Look at him," I say pointing to someone in the queue. "There's no way he's getting in with those sandals. Look at that guy's T-shirt. No collar, no chance."

I sense the bouncer is growing a little irritated. I call fellow writer Kevin McCallum who is already on the inside to explain our predicament. "That's bullshit. He's talking kak. I'm coming out," says no-nonsense Kev.

As it turns out, he's with the manager when I call and they soon appear at the door. The manager waves us in. As we head up the steps, I turn and point to our favourite bouncer. "It was him."

He's not impressed, which pretty much means we are out of the establishment well before anyone needs throwing out.

Cementing his place

It's quarterfinal week in the RWC 2003 and the travelling media cracks an invite to lunch with the Bok team management. We are supposed to come to their hotel but we're suspicious. Why, after an unpleasant tour in which they waged a them-and-us campaign, would they want to booze us up?

On Saturday, you see, the Boks are due to meet the All Blacks at the Telstra Dome (Docklands Stadium) and the portents for them are a little grim. The last year of coach Rudolf Straeuli's rein has been deeply unpalatable on and off the field.

Some folk, however, can't pass up the opportunity for a free lunch and we all head to their hotel. We are outside on the terrace and it is a fine day. We don't see much of Straeuli but assistant coach Rudy Joubert has been at the wine. He is laughing rather boisterously and we are not sure what he is laughing at should be considered funny.

He is seated at another table so we are not too bothered. I'm sitting with Grote and a few others. Our interaction with the team management has been negligible until Joubert breezes past.

He looks at Grote and says. "Het jy die sementlorrie ingesluk?" (Did you swallow the cement truck?) We aren't sure what we should be more surprised about, that he got so hammered or what he had just said.

Mistaken, again

My mate Grote has had to put up with a lot. Early during the 2003 RWC in Perth someone who had been staring at him eventually came across and asked, "Aren't you Jeff Moloi [former television sports news reader]?"

The rest of us found it hilarious that someone in Aussie would know Jeff. Grote, though, was unimpressed and his sulk deepened every time we called him Jeff in the ensuing weeks.

He can be a sensitive fella and the teasing had mildly subsided by the time we reached Melbourne for the quarterfinals of the tournament. Besides, by then we had reached the serious part of the tournament.

On an excursion – window shopping more than anything else – we wandered into Nike Town (a mega store dedicated to the brand with a swoosh). We didn't spend long and as we got to the exit and turned right a bloke walking in the opposite direction checked us out. I was convinced the bloke was looking at Grote and so it proved. We were barely 20 metres down the sidewalk when the local charged after us.

"Hello, hello," he kept saying as he closed in.

We turned and he asked Grote, "Aren't you Lawrence Sephaka?"

By the next time we arrived in Australia a year later we had almost forgotten how easily Aussies misidentify people from the African continent. This time we were on Tri-Nations duty and our travelling pack was considerably smaller. Three of us walked into a bar that boasted some pool tables. The aim was to have a quick beer before we set off in search of food.

While we played a quick round I noticed some blokes staring at us. They weren't sizing us up; they just looked curious. Once we were done we headed for the door. One of the blokes ran after us and asked Simnikiwe Xabanisa. "Are you Trevor?"

He was met with an indignant "No!"

Sim tried to analyse the folly of the young man's ways, while the rest of us just chuckled at his expense. We did wonder why someone would randomly enquire if Sim was Trevor. Who was Trevor anyway?

With that question still teasing me, I turned to Google the next morning and searched for famous Australians called Trevor. The search engine sprang to life but produced nothing.

With the mystery unresolved, we make up a story that maybe "Trevor" is a dreadlocked contestant in Australia's *Idols*.

If the reference to Trevor riled Sim, more Australian quirks came at his expense later in the week. It's late and we are having a beer in the Burswood Casino and Resort.

The place is packed. We're in the casino but our only business here is beer. We have found a good vantage point from where we can observe the floor. Close by, however, two Aboriginal women have fixed their gaze on us. Not just that, they're talking about us and happy for us to know that they are talking about us.

Now the drinkless women are nudging closer. We try not to make too much eye contact, but soon they are next to us. Despite their physical proximity, we stay in our lane. They now start commenting on what we're talking about. It is clear that we are not going to buy them drinks but that reality hasn't yet set in. So, desperate to draw some reaction from us, one of them blindsides Sim by quickly running her fingers through his dreadlocks. He turns to her; he's pissed off.

She, however, is in a state of semi euphoria as she informs her friend: "I told you. It's like two-minute noodles."

Chester missing

It had been an absolute marathon but it was all now coming to a climactic end. The Springboks' end-of-year tour of Argentina, Ireland, Wales and England, which included mid-week matches and an additional week in Cardiff for a match against the Barbarians, had been a real test of strength and endurance.

We would never see the likes of it again. The Boks had finished their tour with a wonderful exhibition of attacking rugby, beating a similar offence-minded Barbarians team 41–31 in Cardiff.

Although it had been an enjoyable tour, we were all relieved that it was over. In fact, the entire tour group, including the media, had taken things down a notch following the Springboks' defeat to England eight days before.

It's Sunday night and the boys are keen to celebrate the end of the tour. Cardiff is a party town and it isn't difficult to find an establishment willing to pull a pint, so we all scatter in different directions but within a half-kilometre radius. By the time the pubs start closing, members of the touring party staying at the Marriott Hotel, which is very conveniently located in the city's party district, start trickling back in. No one, it seems, heads for the lifts.

Everyone seems to take a sharp right into the hotel bar, which is just beyond reception. The mood is boisterously festive. It is the end of a long season in which the Boks played 12 Tests and four midweek matches and one against the Baabaas. They had also experienced a change of coach halfway through the season when Nick Mallett was relieved of his duties after he questioned the exorbitant price of Test-match tickets.

Surprisingly, it was Harry Viljoen who was brought in from the cold and presided over this long tour, which he hoped would herald a new dawn for Springbok and South African rugby. Viljoen was trying to revolutionise Springbok rugby by playing a game and selecting players that could break down the near-impenetrable defensive systems of the day. The players thus had a lot to take on board on that tour, but now they could look forward to a December break.

Some of my colleagues and I are standing near the right-hand corner of the bar counter, a good place from which to observe the rest of the bar. Apart from having a decent view of the rest of the establishment without turning your head, you can also see who is likely to come through the door next.

The drinks are flowing and it seems the ideal way to end the tour. I have, however, developed the uneasy feeling that the person right in the corner where the bar counter meets the wall is staring at us, me in particular. I ignore it at first but later that unease causes me to turn in his direction and give the soon-to-be octogenarian a curious look.

He mumbles something. I lean in, asking, "Excuse me?"

He leans forward and, with an admiring smile, says: "I've been following your career from the very start."

I'm mildly perplexed before the penny drops. He's under the impression I'm a RWC 1995 hero who had played his 27th and final Test against Wales on the left wing two weeks earlier.

I shouldn't have delivered a sarcastic reply but I do. "I didn't realise you get *The Argus* here."

Something stirs in Lake Taupo

Sometimes, however, things turn a little sinister.

Rugby writer Vata Ngobeni – occasionally called "Bcceast!" – was seeing parts of New Zealand his colleagues weren't. For large chunks of the 2011 RWC he was sharing a camper van with fellow scribe Michael "Mickey" Mentz. Depending on the route they were driving on North Island, they were the envy of the travelling pack, but when it came to ablutions we were quite happy with our more formal accommodation arrangements.

They got by though.

When they rolled into Taupo, with its arresting beauty, they were looking forward to not having to drive much for more than a week. The Springboks had set up camp in the picturesque lakeside town on North Island as they had nine days before they had to head off to their next game.

The Springboks' five-star accommodation adjacent to a golf course was to provide welcome respite before their pool match against Samoa in North Harbour and most of the travelling journos were in apartments in reasonable proximity of the lake.

It was a Wednesday night. Ngobeni and Mentz had gone out for one last dop at a place near the local McDonald's. It was a decision that would put Taupo on the map.

"We had two or three dops but then Michael gets onto the dance floor," Ngobeni recalled. "I think there was a little band as well." Ngobeni had taken up position at a high table in the middle of the establishment.

"I went to the bathroom and came back. The cops came in, I think to check if they are going to close an hour early because daylight savings time had kicked in.

"Then the cops came from the bathroom. They asked me what I was doing. I said I was having a dop. Then they asked me about a bag on the floor a little bit away from me.

"I told them I don't know whose bag it is. They said they heard I was trying to sell drugs in the toilet."

Recounting the story, Ngobeni recalls how incredulous he was when they accused him. "I said, 'What? Voetsek, man!'"

They then threatened to detain him.

"Search me," he invited them. They ordered him to go with them. "I said no. They said it wouldn't look good.

People were busy leaving already and I told them I need to tell my friend I have to leave with them. They said no, one of their colleagues will inform him.

"As we drove off, Michael came out looking for me. At the station they tell me the same story again," said Ngobeni.

"There were two guys in the toilet. One was literally passed out over the urinal and the other was throwing up in the toilet.

"They searched me and found nothing. I then had to walk back to that establishment and it's about 700 metres. As we walked across a park the cop then finally asks what I was doing in New Zealand.

"All he knows at that stage is that I'm from South Africa. I'm following the Springboks I tell him. The cop then asks, 'Are you a supporter?' 'No, I'm a journalist,' I tell him. Bloody hell, his eyes went this big," said the scribe making two wide circles with his fingers.

"Then he starts apologising. He says he's sorry but I tell him not as sorry as he is going to be the next day.

"Now he starts calling me sir.

"We get to the other side of the park and Michael runs towards me, saying, 'I think you got lost.'

"Then I tell him what happened. He then starts shouting at the cops, 'You pigs! You arrest the only black man in Taupo. Are you mad?'"

The two then headed to McDonald's. "Mickey then starts telling everyone at McDonald's. All those drunkards then say, 'Them damn pigs.'"

Then they headed to bed.

Mentz, the next morning, shared the story with another journalist. Word got around.

"At practice one of the South African journos reckoned he had just spoken to the *New Zealand Herald* and told them what happened. The paper had asked for a picture of me. We took one with someone's phone.

"Then Mickey goes, 'I'm going to get stuffed up. I was there but the *New Zealand Herald* is going to beat me to the story.' And he was working for the national news agency at the time," Ngobeni chuckled.

"I write the story and send it and of course all hell breaks loose. That fucked up everybody's life.

"Some South African journos only found out about it before the fines meeting that evening. Facebook was working overtime and I get a call from eNCA to say we need to chat.

"Some journos are asking me for an interview and I say, 'No, I'm pissed.'

"That fines meeting was brutal. SA Rugby's chief executive Jurie Roux was presiding over the fines meeting. You could get fined for being too quiet. Soon Roux is labelled Judge and Jurie.

"I remember going to one journo's room to try and relay the story but couldn't.

"I was meant to have a television sit-down also involving the police commissioner but then he bailed out.

"The following morning when we woke up it was all over the front page of the *Herald*. It was bloody huge."

Ngobeni then received a message that "the Maori paramount chief wants to see you."

"When we got there," said Ngobeni shaking his head, "what a spread of sushi. It was in a restaurant in the hotel the Boks were staying in and they effectively shut it down because the paramount chief was coming. His right-hand man started singing in Maori and then told me about the time the paramount chief met Nelson Mandela. He also told me the history of Taupo and how bad it is for this to happen here because they are not *that* kind of people. They were broken."

Ngobeni doesn't know what happened to the cop who took him in for questioning. "All I know is that it ended up in parliament. The Maori Federal Party called me in to have a chat at one of their seminars.

"I said 'I can't, we've got our own problems in our country.'"

Ngobeni then got a call from Andy Colquhoun, SA Rugby's communications manager and Springbok media manager on that tour. "He tells me to meet them at Sky City for a meeting with the chief of police," said Ngobeni.

"I get there and I had a massive babbelas. Oregan Hoskins [then president of SA Rugby] walks down. He introduces the police chief. 'Bill, meet Vata. Vata, meet Bill.'

"He also introduces me to the IRB [International Rugby Board] chief executive Mike Miller but then I notice Peter de Villiers walking off.

"He gets into a car and is gone."

The meeting had already happened.

"Oregan tells me it was more like The Peter de Villiers Meeting. Peter told the police commissioner, 'Do you know where we come from? Do you know how our people suffered under apartheid? And we thought New Zealanders were our friends. Clearly you are not our friends. Do you know who that guy is?'

"Bill said to me: 'Whatever you want. We'll make sure you'll have a comfortable World Cup.'

"That's how I got to use that Land Rover."

Ngobeni reckoned that once he got to Auckland everyone was looking at him. "In one grocery store this old lady came up to me. 'Are you that chap that …?' I just said, 'Yes.'

"She said: 'We are not all like that you know. They have a special breed down there.'"

Lingering tension

What the South African media have become increasingly aware of is the undercurrent of racial tension in New Zealand: how the different racial groupings in New Zealand view each other, as well as the way some of them view white South Africans.

New Zealand has a huge South African expat community. In Auckland they largely reside in the northern part of the city towards North Harbour, with large Samoan communities to the south. They hardly ever mix.

The Springbok tour of New Zealand in 1981 proved a watershed moment for the country. Families were split down the middle about whether the tour should take place or not and the events of that tour are still etched in older Kiwis' consciousness.

On a Bok tour a few years ago a member of the South African media observed an exchange between a local and a South African tourist he would rather forget.

He got back to his hotel around 2.30am after a Test in Wellington.

"I was down at Courtenay Place and I was smashed. I walk into the hotel and there was another South African, a white guy in a Springbok jacket, who was walking that last stretch with me after he came out of Molly Malone's.

"I'd seen him around. As we walked in, he headed towards reception to get another room key or something.

"There was a drunk bloke at the counter who then turned to him. 'You're a fucking Japie, yah?'

"I immediately thought, this is not going to end well.

"I head for the lifts thinking they can sort that out. It has nothing to do with me. But the Kiwi went completely off. He was swearing and making a scene. He reminded the South African, 'If it weren't for us boycotting you guys you'd still …'

"The South African said to him, 'I'm here to support the team. Look at the coach,' which of course just sounded too defensive.

"The Kiwi became extremely abusive. I felt so shit. I'm standing at the lift and I'm thinking, hell, I'm the black guy, and turned back and had to go stand up for the white South African.

"I went to tell the Kiwi, 'Hey, it's not like that … Mandela, *Sarafina* and all the rest.'"

Things didn't quiet down and he went to bed thinking, why is this my job now?

Vata Ngobeni tells the story of how he stopped at a garage close to North Harbour Stadium in the days following his big Taupo incident.

"Someone said to me, 'Don't look behind you,'" he recalls.

"Of course I turned around and there were about 50 to 60 blokes dressed like minstrels you'd find in Cape Town. They spotted me and proceeded to tell me how racist New Zealand really is."

On another occasion, also during the RWC, another black reporter was cornered by a coloured bloke who had left Cape Town behind:

"He was having a proper go. Then he gets teary eyes and next thing reckons it cost him about R250 000 to move his shit over and he can't afford to move back.

"He then says something I found really interesting. He says, 'I'm coloured. When these folks look at me they think I'm Maori.' I asked him, 'Does that make you a second-class citizen?' And he says, 'Ja.'

"I thought, what were you thinking? That must be heartbreaking.

"The guy then says, 'I'm stuck here. There is nothing I can do. My kids are growing up Kiwi – they've got the fucking accent.'"

No snow in Cardiff

My mate Grote and I walk into a music bar in Cardiff that has a distinct Western theme. The set-up feels a bit like the local Barnyard franchise, but we don't know that when we walk in.

Soon we are sucking on a pint on the upper level looking down at the tables at the bottom and the stage to the left. The band and the vibe have potential, but we are yet to decide whether we'll have a second pint here. While we are contemplating our options two women approach us. Grote is seated closest and the one in front stops and says something in our direction.

I can't hear all of it, so I ask her to repeat. I ask her to repeat again. In slang, she's basically wanting to know where they can get cocaine. Grote and I look at each other, turn to them and shake our heads. Sorry, can't help you. I'm a little incredulous. For all my incredulity, the woman who asked has pluck.

Immediately she asks where we are from and, as Grote answers, she slides in on the bench next to him. Soon we have to repeat that we do not have or know where she can find what she's looking for.

They get up as their three friends make their way up the steps, and ask whether we want to join them at a place nearby. Why not? They know the place better than us. Or do they?

We are barely outside, though, when one of them makes a wailing sound. She's wearing high heels and has gone over on her ankle. She can walk, but is clearly in pain. The decision is made: we go one way and they go home, still without cocaine.

Filter or plain

It's autumn in Paris and Grote is in and out of the Indiana Café next to a big roundabout in Saint-Claude. He has the urge to puff on his Gauloises and has to leave the establishment to do so. This habit often means our food orders are delayed or, when there is uncertainty over a certain meal, it isn't immediately resolved.

Grote also has the habit of putting waiting staff on the spot. He would ask in his gruff voice how big a certain steak is as if the person wearing the apron had sourced the produce.

Some staff, however, give as good as they get. Grote is rather bemused when a waitress at the Indiana Café retorts, "Are you Barry White?"

Eight
Being There

Those lucky enough to follow the Springbok team get a front-row seat for which many would cut out an organ. We get to watch matches in far-flung places and see parts of the world we might not have otherwise. We may see the game up close and, when we can find the time, take in the sights, but we also have to put up with the locals' peculiarities.

It all remains a thrill.

The other World Cup

CHANCES ARE YOU may not have heard of the Colin Elsey Shield.

Elsey was a pioneering rugby photographer who died after suffering a stroke aged 64 in 2003. He co-founded the Colorsport agency in 1969 and was responsible for some iconic rugby images, most notably perhaps for the way he froze British and Irish Lions prop Fran Cotton in time:

Cotton was covered in mud from head to toe in Wellington and the image perfectly captured rugby of that era.

Known around the rugby fraternity as "Big C" because of his hulking frame, Elsey passed away a month or so before the 2003 RWC. It was thus decided to arrange a media match in his honour and pit northern-hemisphere media against their counterparts in the south. A date was set during the knockout stages of the RWC when writers didn't have to run around like they did in the pool stages.

By then only Australia, New Zealand, England and France remained and, with the Springboks already back home, the South African media contingent had no excuse for not attending. We were to meet somewhere central and board a bus to Coogee, southeast of Sydney. Just after I board I question why it was that I was doing this. The night before had probably been my biggest on this long tour and if I was a cricket score I was feeling round about 66 for six.

The match was to be played at the renowned Randwick Rugby Club, an establishment steeped in history. Established in 1882, the club's World Rugby Hall of Fame inductees include David Campese, Ken Catchpole, Mark Ella, George Gregan and Bob Dwyer.

The match was to be played in four chukkas and other special rules would apply. Given the age and physical condition of the combatants, rolling substitutions would be in operation and full-contact tackling not permitted. To complete a "tackle" you had to place both hands on the ball carrier who had to pass before that happened to avoid surrendering possession.

That meant that scoring was very difficult. The defending team simply spread out in a line across the width of the field and there was no way through.

I'm reluctant to start the game and would go on as a substitute after the first 15-minute chukka. The game is scoreless by the time I make it on, but I'm still not without trepidation. Physical exercise isn't high on my list of priorities right now.

Despite the forgiving rules, I still have to move around quite a bit. I'm pretty knackered and breathing heavily by the time the second chukka finishes but I have to stay on. All I need to do is close down the space of the player opposite me.

And then my worst fear starts to unfold. With the game still delicately poised at nil-all, the bloke next to me doesn't close down the player he is supposed to mark. He then pops a pass to the bloke I'm marking and his advance is at speed and at an angle. It is quite clear he is going to try to outrun me and, with no cover at the back, I realise the game and the honour of all the people who live south of the equator now rests in my hands.

He's got half a yard on me and now I need to sprint like I have not for at least a decade. I need to carefully time my lunge for him because I need to plant two palms on his body. When I do, I get my right hand on his right buttock and my left on his left leg.

That crisis averted – but I now have a new one. After the "tackle", I stay down. I'm absolutely spent.

When I eventually get to my feet I don't have to signal that I need to come off. Everyone can see it. My replacement comes on and I proceed like a sloth on sleeping pills. When I get to my teammates on the side of the field I am given an energy drink, which I barely have the strength to open. I voluntarily collapse onto my back, spent. I close my eyes, shielding them from the sun. My teammates are concerned.

"You okay, mate?" one asks.

I give the thumbs up and another asks, "You sure?"

My South African colleagues have a chuckle because some of them are partly responsible for the state I'm in.

Finally, I get up – just in time to see the game finish in a 0–0 stalemate.

Handshakes all round and then it is time to clean up.

Our invite suggests we're in for a "BBQ", but first I need to decide whether I can have a beer. The shame of not having a beer would just be too great.

I get food too and join a few South African writers at a large round table. Soon the esteemed Welsh writer and commentator Eddie Butler joins our group. He also played 16 Tests for Wales at No. 8.

As we tuck into our steaks and salad, a seasoned South African writer, no doubt impressed by the new arrival's hulking frame, turns to Eddie as he takes a sip of his beer. "You must have played a game or two?" he enquires.

Kevin McCallum, the offender's colleague, and I are under the table with laughter.

Eight years later I have to buy boots. An invite has dropped. It's time again to contest the Colin Elsey Shield.

"The match will be full contact, intended to be fun, and rolling subs will be encouraged to cater for every level of fitness and ability! The evening will also include a BBQ and use of the clubhouse bar," reads the invite.

The northern-hemisphere side will be captained by *Rugby World* editor Paul Morgan and the south by Dave Campbell, former *Rugby News* editor in New Zealand.

This time it will be played at an equally august venue.

The Ponsonby Rugby Club isn't just in an impressive setting. It too has produced international players of the highest order. It was formed in 1874 and is the longest-running grassroots club in New Zealand with more than 50 teams now. The club has a museum with rugby artefacts going back to an All Blacks jersey from 1905.

I am in no better physical shape than I was eight years earlier, but at least I don't have the raging hangover that afflicted me in Sydney.

Former top ref Paddy O'Brien arrives. He's going to officiate the match and the moment he steps onto the field the verbal abuse starts.

"Oh, Paddy, when last did you ref a game?" someone asks the then International Rugby Board referees bigwig.

"Paddy, you can't favour the south," a northerner advises the Kiwi.

I doubt it would have helped our cause if he was a little one-eyed that day. The North is fired up, having lost 24–10 in Paris four years earlier.

They even trash talk.

They clearly have more players who are currently active. Their flyhalf is built like a brick outhouse and every time he gets the ball he runs straight and hard and gains metres that present the north with valuable momentum.

In the second half I get the opportunity to break our duck. By far our best player, Liam Napier from New Zealand's Fairfax Media, creates an overlap and throws me a pass on the left wing. I need to run at speed to be able to beat the defence and score in the corner.

I'm half a yard off the pace and, instead of adroitly gathering the ball and tucking it under my left arm, I spill the ball forward.

You really need to do some exercise, I chastise myself as I run back, but there seems to be a mild commotion on the other side of the field where most of the onlookers have gathered.

One South African journalist starts shouting, "Chester! Chester!" every time I touch the ball and a local who takes exception takes him to task.

Ah well, I think. They can sort it out.

North continues to dominate and our resistance is broken. Paddy O'Brien blows the final whistle and we lose resoundingly with a score of 34–0.

Indomitable spirit

Mendoza is a tricky destination to get to. In 2012, for instance, the Springboks had to board four flights before they touched down in the city in western Argentina. They had narrowly beaten Argentina in Los Pumas' inaugural match in the Rugby Championship before flying from Cape Town to Johannesburg the day after the match. It was then on to São Paulo and Buenos Aires before the final leg to Mendoza.

Such exhaustive journeys take a physical toll, and mental anguish is never far away, even if you're flying business class. The more your luggage has to be moved from one aircraft to the next, the greater the risk of it not arriving with you at the final destination.

That's exactly what SA Rugby vice president James Stofberg discovered when he walked up to the luggage carousel in Mendoza. It is likely that that is the only active carousel, so if you don't spot your bag immediately you know there's trouble. In fact, by then you should really have spotted your bag on the tractor-drawn carriage that chugged towards the terminal.

Back then SA Rugby's three top officials – the president, deputy president and vice president – would alternate accompanying the team on their overseas travels. This was Stofberg's turn but the vastly experienced administrator and coach's trip started on the worst possible note. Stofberg is well travelled. He even coached Russia, but the missing bag was going to test his usually laidback exterior.

As SA Rugby's representative official, Stofberg arrived in Mendoza wearing his navy-blue jacket, which he was likely to also wear when on official duty. Of course, once he checked in at the stately Diplomatic Suite Hotel, with its wonderful vistas of the eastern slopes of the Andes, he was off shopping.

For the rest of the week we'd see him in either a jersey or his navy-blue jacket. We'd politely enquire about his bag and whether he'd had an update about its whereabouts. The imperturbable Stofberg would just shrug his shoulders. Thankfully, he had his trusty blazer with him, so was sufficiently armed to attend some of the official functions lined up for that week.

Outgoing ambassador to Argentina Tony Leon was going out with a bang. Two breakfasts, one with the team and the other with business leaders, was arranged for the Park Hyatt Hotel. Then there was an SA Rugby Legends dinner in honour of Joost van der Westhuizen, as well as a pre-match dinner the night before the Test.

The SA Rugby Legends dinner was a particularly poignant affair. Van der Westhuizen, although by then diagnosed with motor-neuron disease, would not yield to its associated torpor. He still had a zest for life and was an enthusiastic traveller when the occasion demanded it.

It would have been the first time those in the rugby fraternity in Argentina would witness Van der Westhuizen's physical decline. That he would have agreed to undertake that long journey surprised many, but those who knew him well hardly raised an eyebrow.

That night Van der Westhuizen spoke matter of factly about his plight, but it was his indomitable spirit that barely left a dry eye in the house. Even though motor-neuron disease had drastically affected his speech, his views carried weight. "It will be different. Argentina will be better," said Van der Westhuizen about the improvement he anticipated. "I think they will be much more disciplined and that will present a greater challenge for the Springboks," he added.

"[Joost] is fighting a massive battle," said Bok captain Jean de Villiers. "It puts into perspective what we do. Our battles are nothing to what he has to go through every second of his life. He is a great inspiration and remains someone you can look up to," continued De Villiers whose own career and that of the erstwhile captain overlapped just once on the playing surface before the 2003 RWC.

Going out in song

The 1999 RWC was building to its crescendo. It had been a marvellous tournament, with Wales hosting but matches were played in Ireland, England, Scotland and France.

From the cavernous 80 000-seater Stade de France on the outskirts of the metropolis that is Paris to 6 000-capacity Galashiels, with its population of not much more than 10 000, the RWC was celebrated far and wide.

And that was the only problem with it. The one constant criticism of that RWC is that it was geographically too spread out and it didn't feel like Wales were really hosting it. The Welsh are immensely proud of their rugby heritage so the sense that their RWC was somehow a little diluted did not sit well with them.

The spread-out RWC certainly worked for me because I was assigned to a roving role. Back then newspapers still had a few bob and our group deployed three writers to the 37-day tournament. One writer would focus on the Springboks for the morning papers in the group, while the other would service the afternoon editions.

I would focus my attention on the opponents the Springboks were likely to meet in the quarterfinals and it was destined to be one helluva knock-out match, with the Springboks likely to clash with either New Zealand or England.

The All Blacks were the form team in the world and they had handed the Springboks a drubbing in the last match they played in Pretoria earlier that year, while England had similar bragging rights following their defeat of the Springboks in November of the previous year. Both were heavily favoured to beat South Africa in the quarterfinal, with the Springboks' star widely considered to be on the wane since their 18-match unbeaten run snapped by England the year before.

My brief meant I had to report mostly on clashes at

Twickenham, where England would play the bulk of their matches, but I also had the opportunity to sneak out of town on day trips to Bristol and Huddersfield.

The New Zealand game against Tonga at Ashton Gate was quite something even before the match, with both teams given the green light to perform their respective hakas. The match officials, perhaps in anticipation of fireworks, had strategically positioned themselves on the halfway line, the teams just inside their respective 10-metre lines.

The All Blacks went first and I had never seen their kamate haka stared down the way the Tongans had. When it was their turn the Tongans, who were clearly whipped up into a frenzy, edged forward with intent, almost encroaching on the halfway line when the officials stepped in but by then the teams were face to face.

There were fireworks in the game too with Christian Cullen and Tana Umaga both tackled within an inch of their existence. The All Blacks' class, however, prevailed.

Huddersfield's McAlpine Stadium provided a splendid backdrop for New Zealand's 101–3 crushing of Italy. It took me so long to add up the score that I had to run for and then leap into the last train back to London.

There was also time to watch Australia beat Ireland in Dublin, and although that was a journey I'd rather forget thanks to the staff at British Midland, the destination is well worth visiting considering that Dubliners are friendly and feisty, and that always makes for memorable evenings.

The pool featuring New Zealand and England was always going to be decided by their clash at Twickenham and as you'd expect the British papers wanted to avenge their team's ignominious exit at the hands of the All Blacks four years earlier. But, for all the hype, when they finally met at Twickenham, the match was a damp squib, with Jonah Lomu again delivering a thunderous performance against the wilting Red Roses. This meant that England now had to follow the low road if they wanted to reach the RWC final. First they had to beat Fiji to earn the right to face South Africa in the quarterfinal proper, and as it turned out they went on to negotiate that hurdle with aplomb.

On to Paris, where old rivalries would be resumed, albeit for the first time on neutral ground. The Springboks had historically held sway over England but they were seen as a team in decline.

Now we too were getting caught up in the hype. I got to swear in an intro, in relating comments attributed to former England coach Dick Best. The coach had a particular description of England flank Neil Back, who had cut a talismanic figure in the Red Rose pack.

"Je l'appelle l'éleveur de porc parce qu'il tient ses mains dans la merde." Best was being quoted in a French paper and I thought it useful for one of my feature pieces ahead of the clash. "Neil Back reminds me of a pig farmer. Always crouched over with his hands in the shit," Best said about Back's propensity to turn balls over at the ruck, or just be a nuisance. And on match day, Back's surname was quite fitting because that was the part of his anatomy on which he spent most of the afternoon as the Bok forwards fronted up.

The match will forever be remembered for Jannie de Beer's five drop goals, which helped secure a famous win for the Boks. The five drops remain a record.

As De Beer landed his second drop, the two British writers in front of me in the press tribune each wore a frown as they looked at each other. When the third landed, one muttered audibly to himself, "What's this then?" And when Scots referee Jim Fleming raised his arm to signal a fourth successful drop off De Beer's boot the same hack turned to his colleague wearing a deeper frown. "They should outlaw this thing," he bristled. Finally, when the fifth landed, he was beavering away at his keyboard and he gave England a right royal wallop in his review of the game.

It was back to Cardiff for the third place play-off in which Breyton Paulse scored the Boks' only try in South Africa's triumph over New Zealand. The match felt hollow but the Boks, especially their coach Nick Mallett, were delighted.

Bok coaches will take any win over the All Blacks, and this meant two consecutive defeats for the All Blacks who now had to fly home and face the music. Coach John Hart was public enemy number one and he was crucified on radio talk shows back home.

As it turned out, the RWC final between Australia and France failed to capture the imagination. After the Tricolores beat the All Blacks in the semifinals, there had been a fear that they had popped the corks on their Champagne a week too soon and the Wallabies, who miraculously only conceded one try in the whole tournament (Juan Grobler for the United States), romped home 35–12 to lift the Webb Ellis Cup for the second time.

With our copy of the final filed, we headed into the teeming streets of Cardiff. Even if the hosts weren't involved in the climax, for the locals this was going to be a huge night of celebration for hosting a successful RWC.

I was with my then Independent Newspapers colleagues Gavin Rich and Mike Greenaway. We had been away from home for over 40 days and although our accommodation was 65 kilometres away in Swansea, we were keen to be part of this party.

Problem was we couldn't get in anywhere – all the bars were packed, with long queues outside. But then, somewhere near John Batchelor's statue, we spotted a bar where it was absolutely pumping inside, the queue outside, curiously, not that long. So we headed there, our laptop bags still dutifully dangling from our shoulders.

The doorman smiled and soon we were in, heading for the bar through the very heavy traffic. There we ordered two draught beers and I went for a Red Bull and vodka on account of me having to drive later.

As we turned to survey the sea of humanity we were struck by something ... No wonder the queue was almost nonexistent. The place was almost devoid of women – we had clearly walked into a gay bar.

We chuckled to ourselves but couldn't care less. By the time Manhattan Transfer's "Chanson D'Amour" began to blast through the speakers, we too had our arms raised, firmly swept up in the raucous delirium.

Nine days in Taupo

The Vata Ngobeni episode rather put a damper on the time we spent in Taupo during the 2011 World Cup. The town's tourism office and the mayor, a quirky man I thought would not be out of place at Muriel's wedding, made things interesting over the nine days we spent there.

The Ngobeni episode notwithstanding, the Taupo folk generally look after us well, and we receive an invitation with an extremely officious heading: Taupo District Council and Destination Great Lake Taupo. They had hosted the Welsh media a week earlier and were expecting the Irish a week after the South Africans pass through the door.

On the invite they promise:
- Glass of bubbles on arrival
- Meet our local tourism operators
- Enter to win a magnum of New Zealand champagne

The bit about the "New Zealand champagne" intrigues me, of course, because the effervescent delight is unique to France and a protected trademark. Regardless, the South African travelling pack RSVP en masse. Even though it's a 7am starting time, the breakfast will be free.

Early on we are required to drop our business cards in a bowl and soon the mayor, a short man with a booming voice, takes hold of the microphone. When he finishes – I'm still wondering how they could appropriate the name "Champagne" – my card gets drawn and I win the magnum. I have no idea what to do with it and someone helpfully suggests I just carry it with me wherever I go in Taupo.

The function is pretty much an assembly of tour operators in the area. So we take fliers and business cards before we leave, figuring we can probably engage in some of the activities given the very agreeable time difference between South Africa and New Zealand.

The next day we start making calls. A massage is booked at a luxurious spa, and later that week we climb into a jet boat for an entirely exhilarating ride.

Jet boats, the creation of a Kiwi engineer Bill Hamilton, is a thrill seeker's delight. A water-jet unit delivers a high-pressure "push" from the stern by accelerating a volume of water as it passes through a specialised pump mounted above the waterline inside the boat hull. At breakneck speed, the boat seems to glide over the surface of the water but the thrills really come when there's a sudden rapid turn.

We leave the boat with adrenaline rushing within, and equally soaked on the outside.

By then some of us have made plans to go fishing on the pristine waters of Lake Taupo. For that we require a permit, which the local authority happily issues. We could each catch two or so trout and take it ashore. The plan is to put them over hot coals in the early evening. As you can imagine, by then we are tired of restaurant food and a braai is going to feed the belly and the soul. Some of us are able to hook a few trout and we head for the quay ecstatic with our effort.

The next day four of us clamber into a seaplane to observe Taupo from the air and on another we experience the lake very differently by going out fishing.

By the time we get to Auckland in preparation for the Boks' next match, an article in one of the newspapers reminds us of the lengths the Kiwis will go to if Richie McCaw's men actually win the tournament. A Durex survey has found that a staggering 96 per cent of respondents expect to celebrate an All Black victory by having sex. Ten per cent of the 350 respondents claim that they have had sex at a big sports tournament in the past. Just over a third state that they'd choose Party Central in downtown Auckland as the best public place for a sexual liaison, while 22 per cent indicate that they'd linger at a stadium as part of their celebrations.

Friends and foes

South Africans often claim to be a rugby-mad nation and, to a certain degree, we are, but we don't obsess about it nearly as much as the Kiwis. They have a level of devotion to the sport that far outstrips anything I've encountered. Although the rugby ball is also the object of Welsh affection, in New Zealand love for the sport is next level.

Their obsession hits you the moment you step wearily off the plane. Border-control officials are more than likely to ask you: "Are you here for Saturday's game?" Their eyes usually light up when you answer in the affirmative and then the banter starts. The sound of the stamp in your passport is usually followed by a mildly sarcastic "Good luck on Saturday."

Once you've removed your bag from the luggage carousel, you have to make your way through customs where the process repeats itself. At this point, however, don't be found in possession of biltong, no matter how it's packaged. On my most recent visit a travelling companion had to part with three kilograms of game biltong.

If you then get into a taxi or minibus shuttle, the driver – once they've discovered you're a "Safrican" – will interrogate you about the team the Bok coach has assembled. This will happen irrespective of whether the driver was born in Denpasar, Dhaka or Delhi. And by the time you get to your hotel you are travel weary in every sense, but you are often likely to face the same line of interrogation when you check in.

There are exceptions. I was surprised to find an Indian-looking woman at the wheel of the taxi I slid into on Courtnenay Place in Wellington early one morning. She must have been in her mid-sixties, I figured. Soon she wanted to know whether I had introduced "Him" into my life. At first I was confused, but then the penny dropped. So I told her that, apart from John (Jameson) and his son, I had not firmed up any friendships that evening. She was as confused as I had been a little earlier.

A reporter on his first Springbok tour soon discovered how much the Kiwis revere the game.

He returned to his hotel room in Christchurch in 2007 to get some work done but on his arrival discovered that a middle-aged member of housekeeping was still tidying up. He apologised for interrupting her but urged her to continue what she was busy with while he got on with what he was supposed to.

He noticed, though, that she seemed a little distracted. She was eyeing the Springbok scarf that was spread across his bed. Eventually, she could no longer contain her curiosity. "Are you with the Springbok team?" she politely enquired.

He explained that he was from South Africa and that he was part of the travelling media. She found this fascinating and wanted to know more about the team before revealing that she had watched some of the matches of the Springboks' tour of New Zealand in 1981.

The reporter couldn't believe it. But she went a step further. She told him she could name the Springbok starting line-up for all three Tests played on that tour. The reporter thought this impossible, so he turned to his laptop and found a website that chronicles the Springboks' Test history. She started naming them.

She started with the first Test of that series, which happened to be played in Christchurch: "Fullback Gysie Pienaar, wings Ray Mordt and Darius Botha. Centres Danie Gerber and Willie du Plessis, flyhalf Naas Botha and scrumhalf Divan Serfontein."

The reporter was impressed, but surely she couldn't keep this up ..."Loose forwards Rob Louw, Theuns Stofberg and Eben Jansen. Locks Louis Moolman and Hennie Bekker. Front row Hempies du Toit, Robert Cockrell and Henning van Aswegen."

With the team that lost 14–9 under her belt, she then went on to name the much-changed line-up for the second Test the Springboks won at Athletic Park in Wellington. The pack was barely recognisable from the first Test, with only Theuns Stofberg and Louis Moolman retaining their positions in the starting line-up. But she knew all those changes, as well as the single but significant change in the back line where Gerrie Germishuys replaced Darius Botha. Germishuys went on to score the only try of the second Test as the Boks prevailed 24–12 to level the series.

By now, of course, it came as no surprise to the reporter that she named the three changes the Boks made to their team for that fateful final Test they lost 25–22.

Jannes LabuShame

The ping sound means we've reached the ground floor. The lift doors separate but as I'm about to step forward I immediately stop. The man in his mid-forties, keen to enter, looks familiar. Just as his name registers, a more muscular man to his right stretches out his left arm to prevent the doors from closing.

"You coming, mate?" he asks. Emile Heskey is basically imploring me to snap out of the involuntary trance I have slipped into. It's dawned on me that the Liverpool team has checked into the swanky Royal Garden Hotel in Kensington, the same hotel I have been calling home for the last six days.

Heskey, the Liverpool striker, has Phil Thompson, a club legend and assistant coach, to his right. I vacate the lift and turn towards the lobby. Yes, the team is busy checking in and now I have to come to terms with the fact that Liverpool and the Springboks are in the same hotel.

It is Friday, the night before the Springboks are due to play England at Twickenham and Liverpool meet Fulham at Craven Cottage. I see the Liverpool manager, Gerard Houlier, and the rest of the team either completing check-in or dragging bags towards the lift. In all the human traffic I don't see the French rugby scribe I'm looking for. Serge Magnificat – I've always thought he has a wonderful byline – had suggested earlier that we go out for a bite, and I figure he has probably made his way upstairs to the bar on the mezzanine level.

First I greet television commentator Hugh Bladen and former Springbok wing Syd Nomis, who are seated in wonderfully luxurious wingback chairs before I head for Serge. He is with an English scribe. My former colleague Gavin Rich joins us and on the Englishman's insistence the four of us head for Earl's Court to what is apparently the best French bistro in London.

Already Gavin and I are a little concerned what this might do to our tour allowance but we only have two nights to go on the Springboks' November 2002 tour of Europe. The French are expecting us and we are immediately shown down a spiral staircase to the bar and cellar.

We are simply asked, "Red?, white?" and within seconds we are quaffing away. Naturally, we get chatting to the owner who matches the look of a retired prop and restaurateur. He's charming and the conversation and the wine eat effortlessly into time.

Suddenly the owner looks up at the staircase and with a wide smile welcomes the latest arrival. It's the legendary former French fullback Serge Blanco who, 11 years after his international retirement, also has the girth of a prop. He greets everyone warmly and soon enough the conversation is flowing as easily as the wine. Heaven knows how many times they top up our glasses, because by now Gavin and I are growing weary.

Eventually someone summons us; our table is ready. We drag ourselves up the stairs and right at the back there is a round table with a multi-tiered serving tray in the middle – basically a tower of seafood, and Gavin and I immediately develop indigestion at the thought of what this could come to.

I try to draw comfort from the fact that the next day is my birthday and, given our commitments at Twickenham, there will be no time to celebrate. I don't generally celebrate my birthday so I don't bother telling the others.

We feast on what should really be called Neptune's banquet before, following a splendid meal, some of us empty our wallets.

We all go our separate ways, but the next day all roads lead to Twickenham. The Boks are trying to salvage some pride after abysmal performances against France in Marseille, where they lost by a record margin 30–10 and against Scotland where they set another all-time low in losing 21–6.

To be fair, Rudolf Straeuli's team had been beset by

injury and he has had to call up reinforcements almost from the moment the Boks arrive in Europe. He is desperate for his team to beat England because that could serve as a psychological blow ahead of the RWC match in Perth the following year.

But, on a typically chilly and overcast afternoon in southwest London, the Boks find themselves on the backfoot from the get-go. Clive Woodward's England team is in an advanced stage in their development as RWC challengers and the Boks are seen as no more than a small speed bump to the runaway chariot.

England is already well in the ascendancy by the time Bok Jannes Labuschagne lock drops his left shoulder into England flyhalf Jonny Wilkinson. To compound matters, the tackle is late – well after the ball has left the superb flyhalf's boot – and referee Paddy O'Brien has little choice but to show Labuschagne the red card. The lumbering No. 4 is enthusiastically boo-ed as he departs.

Now the Boks' job has become infinitely more difficult. With just seven Bok forwards to plug the holes, England continues to maraud upfield. In one move, their rolling maul sees them back pedal the Boks into their own 22-metre area.

An already loud England fan seated back left of the press box loses the plot. "That's it. That's it. Kill them. Kill them!" he exclaims, causing some of us to rubber neck to his location.

The Boks try to be belligerent but all they can manage is to resort to over-zealous physicality to try to unsettle the hosts. Somehow, they succeed in making an already unfolding trainwreck look worse. England pile on the misery and when O'Brien eventually blows the final whistle the score reads 53–3 to England.

It would be the worst Bok Test I witness in the flesh.

The venues

Watching the national teams play has taken me to every continent except Antarctica. When you travel to different locations, it is quite staggering how facilities that may be deemed fit for Test-match rugby in one location are soundly rejected in others.

Venues vastly differ and listed below are some I've been fortunate enough to visit.

Stade de France (Paris, France) – The spaceship in the city's northern wastelands is hard to beat for atmosphere. I've watched the Tricolores play there and it's great but watching Les Bleus run out there is simply next level.

Twickenham (London, England) – Twickenham (or HQ, as the locals call it) is a concrete monstrosity that always looks as cold as ice. One of my worst rugby memories unfolded there on a cold November afternoon in 2002. The walk from and to Twickenham station is always a treat.

Principality Stadium (Cardiff, Wales) – I'm rather fond of this stadium, especially the pre-match build-up before the anthems, which include a male choir and a rendition of *Delilah* as belted out by 80 000-plus Welsh souls. It's something else.

Lansdowne Road/Aviva Stadium (Dublin, Ireland) – The old venue was quite frankly a fire risk, but Aviva Stadium is splendid, albeit with some architectural quirks.

Murrayfield (Edinburgh, Scotland) – This is another venue that cheers you before kick-off. They can really spare the travelling journos the haggis for lunch though.

Stade Vélodrome (Marseille, France) – The fairly recently revamped stadium played host to Jean de Villiers and Bakkies Botha's debuts. One left the field injured fairly early on, while the other was yellow carded on a night the Boks froze in front of the French and the mistral chilled bones in the stands.

Subiaco Oval (Perth, Australia) – This stadium is in a residential area but is an absolute nightmare from which to hail a taxi once your work is done. The Nando's located a few blocks away is to be avoided, not because of the food, but rather the over-enthusiastic Saffas.

Eden Park (Auckland, New Zealand) – The All Blacks' fortress is one of rugby's cathedrals. Somehow, it isn't as imposing or hostile as the Kiwis make it out to be.

Jade Stadium (Christchurch, New Zealand) – Cold and towering on one side, this stadium was decommissioned after being ravaged by the 2011 earthquake. A particularly uncomfortable chair meant that my first visit there was painful.

Aami Stadium (Christchurch, New Zealand) – This is a makeshift facility on agricultural show grounds, and really shouldn't host any big events. For Pete's sake, the press conferences take place in a tent and the change rooms are almost off site.

Westpac Stadium (Wellington, New Zealand) – Although it's shaped like a cake tin, the wind still finds a way into the stadium. Someone should also educate the ushers about how to get to the media centre.

Forsyth Barr Stadium (Dunedin, New Zealand) – This indoor venue isn't big but that helps generate atmosphere. The roof certainly helps with the acoustics, but kickers still find a deceptive breeze.

Suncorp Stadium (Brisbane, Australia) – This is an extremely functional stadium with a wide concourse and uninterrupted views from wherever you're seated.

Stadium Australia (Sydney, Australia) – Located in Homebush, this stadium is quite a trek from Sydney's Central station. You need to get your timing right when there's an evening kick-off.

Allianz Stadium (Sydney, Australia) – The former Sydney Football Stadium is centrally located next to the Sydney Cricket Ground. This ground is functional and far more intimate than the one in Homebush. Michael Cheika broke a glass door there once.

Telstra Dome (Melbourne, Australia) – The venue of the Springboks' 2003 RWC exit, this stadium located in the Docklands is also enclosed by a roof. It must be a great venue for rock concerts.

Hong Kong Football Club Stadium (Hong Kong) – The home of the Hong Kong Sevens is also a former burial ground. Thankfully, the tombs have been moved because this stadium hosts one of rugby's most raucous events.

Stadio Euganio (Padua, Italy) – Located on the outskirts of Padua, this stadium holds grim memories for the travelling South African media of 2017. Because it is located in the middle of nowhere, we got absolutely drenched struggling to call a taxi.

Petco Park (San Diego, USA) – The baseball ground is the home of the Padres and is conveniently located near San Diego's vibey Gaslamp District. It played host to a few World Sevens Series events before losing out to Las Vegas.

River Plate Stadium (Buenos Aires, Argentina) – The iconic home of the River Plate football team is a concrete monstrosity that is truly inhospitable for visitors. I recall having a nightmare trying to file copy from there and got into trouble for it.

Estadio Malvinas (Mendoza, Argentina) – The stadium is splendidly located in the General San Martin Park. Once inside, however, you can feel the hostility and the Springboks had to settle for a draw on their first visit there in 2012.

Monumental José Fierro Stadium (Tucumán, Argentina) – This is not a stadium for those who are used to being wined and dined in corporate boxes. The locals give you the eye – and some of their saliva if you're not careful.

Sixways Stadium (Worcester, England) – The stadium has seen many improvements since the Boks lost there in 2000. Without accreditation, we talked our way into the venue and were forced off our allocated seats into a corporate suite because of the rain.

Nine

It Will Never Be the Same

Rugby and the industry in which I work have irrevocably changed over the last while. The game, so strongly rooted in amateurism before it turned pro, is barely recognisable from the relatively static action we became accustomed to while growing up.

The media industry meanwhile is increasingly trying to come to grips with advances in technology and the manner in which that has impacted consumers.

Meeting deadlines

TIME MANAGEMENT IS key when you're on tour, especially when you're in a different time zone. Dilly-dallying and procrastinating will leave you having to do things in a rush and your trip can quickly descend into a pit.

Subeditors back home are forever in a flat spin over copy they want in their inbox "yesterday". In fact, in some cases – on Saturdays, for instance – they seem to want the match report before that actual game kicks off. Subeditors and the folk who lay out or design pages, you see, are under increasing pressure. Over the years deadlines have been brought forward to meet pressure at the printing presses and the distribution networks. Everybody is feeling the squeeze and newspapers simply don't get to the places or carry the content they used to.

If a Test match kicks off at 5.10pm, for instance, the early editions of the newspaper are unlikely to carry a match report the next day. Writers are still required to submit their match report as close to final whistle as humanly possible – we call it "filing on the whistle" – and some writers are better at it than others. When I joined an Afrikaans daily in 2005 I rather missed the pressure and thrill of having to submit copy on the whistle.

Match reports used to be the barometer by which good sports writers were judged. The ability to distil what they've just witnessed and break it down to the reader in an informative and hopefully entertaining way, while remaining cognisant of the looming deadline, are demands beyond the capabilities of most in the press box.

Most readers of Sunday newspapers would have watched the big match on television the day before, so you need to tell them what they didn't see. At the same time, you can't lose sight of the fact that some folk have not yet watched the match.

The other obligation that needs to be met, and this almost goes without saying, is that those match reports have better be free of errors. With earlier deadlines and an ever-shrinking pool of subeditors in newsrooms, a writer's mistake close to deadline is likely to go undetected and unfixed. And that mistake will feel like ink spilt onto a crisp white shirt.

When you're abroad time differences can be your friend and foe. In that sense, Argentina and the United States present great challenges for writers as the minimum five-hour time difference means your news-gathering day is effectively halved. By the time you get up, half the day is gone in South Africa, which means you try to keep some copy back from the previous day. That is a necessary evil.

Not that operating in Australia and New Zealand is any easier because there you get the sense you are chasing your tail operating effectively a day behind. When touring New Zealand, for instance, any story submitted after 10am (NZ time) is unlikely to make it into South African papers. Sometimes 48 hours pass from the time you hit "send" on your computer before that report is read in a South African newspaper.

The advent of online publications has, however, brought an immediacy to the reporting and consumption of news. Writing for digital platforms and social media has helped even out the playing field, and newspapers with their cast-in-stone deadlines continually have to play catch-up. The idea is thus to provide "bite-sized" content to online publications and the "meat and potatoes" to newspapers.

When you've written about the most pressing issues, you then have to turn your attention to the "how" and the "why" in your newspaper report. That also requires you to come up with fresh angles, which means you are in a constant state of chasing your tail, or even tale.

At least one local newspaper group has a morning and afternoon stream that has to be catered for, over and above requirements for the online publications. In what now seems like the distant past that newspaper group used to send two writers on tour, designating one to each stream. Budgetary constraints have, however, meant only one poor sod now has to file copy around the clock. That person would attend press conferences, barely make it to practice sessions, and then spend the rest of his time in his room beavering away at his keyboard.

You hardly see him otherwise. Writing around the clock like that means the journalist is basically chasing his tail in that futile pursuit of scooping himself.

Get out of Dodge

The company I was working for was going south but staff denial lent our everyday existence a temporary misguided buoyancy.

It was July 2004 and the company I had joined just under a year earlier was haemorrhaging money. *ThisDay*, a wonderful new addition to the newspaper landscape that launched in October 2003, was now in desperate trouble. Owned by Nigerian media mogul Nduka Obaigbena, the publication had assembled some top talent and it was hoped it would raise the bar of South African journalism.

"The newspaper is unique in many ways. It is the first national daily, general interest newspaper to be launched in South Africa," editor Justice Malala said at the time.

I joined the publication in September 2003, amid desperately uncertain times. The launch had been pushed back on at least three occasions, so when I arrived in Perth for the 2003 RWC, two days before the new launch date, it was truly a leap into the unknown. How many writers get sent to a RWC for a publication that doesn't yet exist?

I had to hit the deck running and was required to file copy for the last dummy runs. When I hit "send" for my preview pieces for the 7 October launch edition I had no idea whether those articles would see the light of day. Thankfully, they did.

The first few months were rock 'n roll, but news of cashflow problems at the paper soon surfaced. The paper was gaining readers, but at great cost. Given its wide reach, distribution costs meant that it was proving expensive to get copies to the readers.

It got progressively worse, so by the time I was due to travel to Australia for the Tri-Nations in July 2004, the major concern in the office wasn't overseas travel, but whether salaries would be paid at the end of the month.

Still, though, the editor remained optimistic. I was required to do a costing for the trip, which included the Springboks' one-off Test against the Pacific Islands in Gosford, New South Wales, the Test against the All Blacks in Christchurch a week later, followed by the Test in Perth against Australia.

As my intended departure date grew nearer, it became clearer that I wasn't going to get to the game in Gosford. Never mind, I figured, our focus should be the Tri-Nations Tests anyway.

When I had no word from the editor's office giving me the go-ahead at the start of the following week, I resigned myself to the fact that the trip was off and went to him at the end of the day for confirmation. He invited me into his office. The mood was light and neither of us was too dispirited about the fact that the paper would not be represented in Australasia.

Sure, we were keen to be there, given that the Springboks

had generated so many headlines the year before. They were now under the guiding hand of coach Jake White and it would have been good to see how White got on in the new job.

As Justice and I chatted, a large figure appeared in the doorway. It was Nduka. He wore dark trousers and a loose-fitting white lounge shirt. I found him an affable man, but if you don't know him, the way in which he communicates may come across as curt.

As he extended his arm I got up to greet him, but Justice intervened.

"Don't even greet this man," he said to Nduka.

The barrel-chested Nigerian looked bemused.

"Don't even greet him," Justice repeated. "He's not even supposed to be here."

"Where is he supposed to be?" Nduka demanded to know.

"Australia," came the answer.

"What are you doing here?" asked Nduka, turning to me.

"Well, best you ask Justice," I said pointing to my right.

Justice explained to him that there was no money. Not even in petty cash. Whatever funds there were were being used to cover urgent operational costs. And the line of creditors was getting longer and longer.

"There's no money," Justice reiterated.

Nduka looked slightly bemused as he turned to me. "Excluding the flight, how much do you need?" he asked as he reached into his shirt pocket.

Having again crunched the numbers the week before, they were thankfully still reasonably fresh in my head. I gave him a figure and Nduka produced a wad of rolled-up US dollar bills.

He threw them one by one onto the coffee table as he counted. "Okay, so that will cover your accommodation, meals, taxis and so on?" he double checked.

I looked at the dollar bills strewn across the table and answered, "It should."

The understanding was that Nduka would order the financial director to book the flights and that I should use the cash for all other costs.

Unexpectedly, the next day I was on board Qantas QF64 heading for Sydney and, later, to Christchurch.

Good thing I got to go on the away leg of that Tri-Nations. Although the Boks lost narrowly in Christchurch (23–21, with Doug Howlett breaking Bok hearts in the dying minutes) and Perth (30–26, with Clive Rathbone delivering the dagger this time), the Boks went on to win the competition for the first time since 1998.

A day or two after arriving home from Perth, I headed to the bank to deposit the remaining dollars in my possession. It was not a huge amount, but enough to make the rest of the month enjoyable. The cashier took the notes and slid them under the fluorescent light behind the counter.

"Where did you get this?" he asked with a frown.

I immediately drew a concerned look. From the owner of the company I work for, I told him. I then offered him a little more background.

The cashier then explained that he would ordinarily have to impound the notes and alert the authorities. Some of the notes, he said, had pink markings on them visible only when exposed to the fluorescent light.

I shook my head – in disbelief, but perhaps more for the effect.

He then handed me all the notes and said, "Good luck."

"Thanks," I said, and quietly headed for the revolving door.

A week or so later I was in a coffee shop with a colleague, the effortlessly elegant cricket writer Peter Robinson. He was aware of my predicament.

"Do you have those notes with you?" he enquired.

"Yes, why?"

Robbo shouted across to the owner standing at the counter a little distance away.

"Are you crazy?" I said to Robbo. "I don't want to piss off the Lebanese."

"Don't worry," said Robbo.

"Do you want to buy some dollars?" Robbo asked when he came over to the table.

"For the right price, yah," came the swift reply.

Still a little uneasy with this arrangement, I gave him a figure. And so we swopped cash and I took my last sip of coffee from that shop.

Doomed

And so it had all come to an end. An epic five-week journey that took us to Buenos Aires then Tucumán (Argentina A), back to Buenos Aires (Argentina), off to Cork (Ireland A), Dublin (Ireland), Cardiff (Wales A and Wales), Tewkesbury (England Divisional XV), London (England) and back to Cardiff (the Barbarians).

It was the last time the Springboks undertook a tour that routinely included midweek matches – because of the costs involved, I doubt it is an exercise federation CEOs will sign off on again anytime soon. Lamentably, rugby is about making as much money as possible and midweek matches are a hard sell to broadcasters. Without that additional income, federations are unlikely to sanction the travel of large groups of players who in any event are perennially fatigued.

Tours that include midweek matches are a vestige of the amateur era and although there are whispers that they should be revived, that is going to take some doing in a game becoming increasingly detached from its soul.

On long tours friendships and camaraderie are forged. Players who had been at each other's throats while wearing their provincial jersey become mates and the same certainly applies to the bonds formed between the tourists and the places they visited.

Although the British and Irish Lions, which have become a commercial behemoth, still engage in midweek combat on their quadrennial trips, it is thoroughly disheartening to learn of their plans to shorten their tours.

While travelling on that tour in 2000 we would often remark that it won't get better than what we were experiencing on what felt like an odyssey.

We were right.

Buenos Aires calling

The way we file or transmit copy to the office has changed drastically over the years. When I did my in-service training at the SABC we simply phoned in a story by dictating it to a designated subeditor at the office. That was done on whatever phone you could lay your hands on and often that was a public phone.

If you were out on a really big story, or were heading to a location where a landline may not be readily available, you were issued with a portable phone. It was more or less the size of a 5-kilogram box of wine, but heavier.

We called it the "portie", but is was bloody handy.

When I took up my first fulltime position at *The Argus*, I was introduced to what was known as a "tandy". The tandy basically consisted of a small screen with a tiny keyboard that was attached to a coupler into which you were supposed to fit the receiver of the phone you were using.

You typed your story with only a small portion of the copy visible, and moved the cursor left, right, up or down if you wanted to make amendments elsewhere in your copy. It was very time consuming, and copying and pasting wasn't always an option.

You then had to select between "tone" or "pulse" and type in the number using the keyboard and wait for the device to dial up. It was also wildly temperamental, and you often found yourself calling the office to dictate the story, having wasted an inordinate amount of time – a task made even more difficult from a very small and often tardy if not unresponsive cursor.

Around the mid-1990s laptop computers started surfacing in newsrooms. That revolutionised our business. Writing stories became easier but sending them remained a challenge. You still had to book a Telkom line at the ground where you were to report from and often had to resort to begging another writer for the use of their line, because the Telkom technician didn't pitch up.

My life changed, however, in 1996 when I found a way of transmitting copy written on my laptop via my mobile phone. That was on a cricket tour of the United Kingdom and it soon became the accepted way of filing copy remotely.

Still, though, when you are in a foreign country

communication pitfalls are never far away.

I had an absolute nightmare filing copy from Argentina in 2000. The idea was to write your story, plug the hotel telephone line into your laptop, use the dial-up function on your computer and transmit it after a high-pitched screech and then what sounded like a bouncing sound from a video game. If you don't hear the bouncing sound it usually meant something was wrong and your copy wasn't being transmitted.

That was the story of my first week in Buenos Aires, which in turn led to a fresh problem. Every time I dialled up to Johannesburg the computer connection registered as a call. You can imagine what my phone bill was like by the time I checked out without a single report sent that way.

A staff member from the South African Embassy, where we attended a cocktail party one night, was kind enough to dispatch a technician but he couldn't solve the problem. It was only when I got home a month or so later that one of the IT-wise guys at my office cheerily informed me that the number I'd been dialling had changed.

Trip them up

The Springbok team that travelled to the 2003 RWC was a walking headline. The team that had lurched from one controversy to the next had little chance of lifting the Webb Ellis Cup but remained in the news.

Before the tournament there had been a flare-up between players that had racial undertones, while the nefarious activities at Kamp Staaldraad were yet to be fully aired – enough to take up large swathes of both the front and the back pages during the tournament.

A large South African media contingent had travelled to the tournament. Although sport is not its focus, one of the daily national papers also made plans to get its rugby writer there. He had all his documents in order and his foreign currency was arranged. His wife had applied and was granted leave from her office because she was tagging along to Perth and they had arranged a house sitter to look after their home.

Although the writer had media accreditation for the entire tournament, the understanding was that he was to return home if the Boks failed to beat England in their second pool match in Perth. If the Boks lost to England, they were set to meet New Zealand in the quarterfinals and that was widely considered to be the end of the road for them.

Three days before he was due to depart, however, he received news the newspaper was pulling the plug on the trip.

Sometimes you are left at the mercy of travel agents who have no clue what your requirements are. Yes, you can provide dates of when you need to be where but the devil is very much in the detail.

One writer, admittedly on a very tight budget, spent an entire Tri-Nations tournament in motels located next to the respective airports of Christchurch and Perth. The travel agent had booked him there because they had been the cheapest rooms on offer. However, the money he spent on taxis to get to press conferences, practices and, in fact, matches would have been enough to get him a room in a more civilised part of town.

When I was due to travel to the Tri-Nations in 2004, the travel agent sent through a yet-to-be-confirmed itinerary that would have seen me spend an inordinate amount of time in Gosford on the New South Wales coast.

The Springboks played the Pacific Islands there in coach Jake White's first Test abroad, but the problem with the booking was that it had me fly to Christchurch on the morning of the next Test, against the All Blacks, while the process would have repeated itself the following week when I needed to be in Perth for the Test against the Wallabies.

Somehow, between my office and the travel agent, someone thought I was going on tour just to watch the matches and that writing about the build-up would not be necessary.

That's why I prefer to do my own bookings, which was a big no-no in the past. Media houses, however, are increasingly looking to save a buck and are now more receptive to ideas to save money. Cutting out the intermediary in arranging trips is one way. And, to be honest, for a writer, organising your own trip prevents unnecessary angst. That time is much better spent focusing on work.

Whether you arrange your own trip or whether a travel agent is booking it, one thing has remained constant. Media houses – and I've worked at a few – view sports tours as a grudge payment, even though public interest in the event you are covering is sky high. Very, very rarely are things planned, booked and paid for well in advance. It is usually up to the writer to do last-minute scrambling to make sure their news organisation will be represented.

In fact, as I was writing this I was waiting for final clearance to attend the 2019 RWC in Japan. In May 2019, three weeks after the deadline, I asked to apply for media accreditation.

We had spoken about the RWC months before when flights and accommodation were easier and cheaper to come by.

I'll do my own bookings because it saves money and I know what I need to get the job done. In finding accommodation, the idea is to book it close to where the Springboks are staying, which saves time and most importantly cost. I'll have to attend at least four press conferences there in the week leading up to a match and if it is within walking distance that is first prize.

Companies have, with great alacrity, slashed the costs of sending their writers abroad.

Photographers, who for some time have been an endangered species in newsrooms around the world, are hardly ever sent on tour. Media houses instead use what is supplied by agencies. We tend to book the cheapest flight, which sometimes means we have to fly into the northern hemisphere to get to, say, New Zealand, and stay in hotels that have three stars or fewer. I, for instance, flew to Singapore to get to Christchurch in 2016 and was on the ground for less than 48 hours before having to fly back. That's like playing pinball with the body's built-in clock.

Per diem – or daily allowances – have also been brutalised. In fact, they are no longer "allowances" but rather an advance signed for by the writer that has to be accounted for upon their return. Having to keep every receipt on a 48-day trip is near impossible and leaves me cold, but bean counters might see it differently.

On an end-of-year tour to Europe in 2017, I made an unpleasant discovery after arriving at Stazione Santa Lucia in Venice. My tour had started in Dublin, then Paris before moving on to Padua, where it reached the halfway mark.

I put the card I was issued for the trip into an ATM and the only paper it dispensed was a slip stating "insufficient funds". The amount I was supposed to be issued for the trip had for some reason been slashed in half. And – surprise, surprise – I was just halfway through the trip.

I reached for my personal bank card, having forgotten about a call I'd received from the bank a week-and-a-half earlier informing me that there had been a fraudulent transaction on that account.

The ATM retained my card and when it came to a sinking feeling, Venice had nothing on me in that moment.

Getting to Japan

The management team's preparations have been meticulous. It all started as far back as 2015 when SA Rugby representatives, like all the other major rugby playing nations, visited the next hosts of the quadrennial RWC tournament.

In 2018 senior national teams manager Charles Wessels and logistics manager JJ Fredericks did more reconnaissance to help finalise travel arrangements to Japan, mostly internal travel that would consist exclusively of high-speed trains between cities, accommodation, gym, recovery and training facilities.

The logistics, however, happens in the background and although they have been in place for a while, the preparation of the team to be battle ready for their seventh assault on the RWC had a stutter or two along the way.

Ideally, top-tier nations prepare in a four-year cycle for the RWC. A coach is installed, usually with a contract that spans that period with some performance clauses, and he in turn puts in place a coaching team that will assist him. Often he can also call on consultants to sharpen particular areas. In the case of SA Rugby, some of the back-up staff may be in their permanent employ.

The performance clause, which is like a sword under which national coaches operate, is often invoked when the team has regressed to a point where progress seems beyond the team's immediate reach.

Allister Coetzee was handed the reins, rather belatedly, after the last RWC and he had to hit the deck running once he was installed in April 2016. He had to play catch-up, but sadly the time lost early in that year was to manifest itself in on-field performances. The Springboks were treading water from the moment they lost to Ireland for the first time on home soil in June that year.

It was an inauspicious start for Coetzee in his first Test in charge and, although the Boks came back to win that series, for the remainder of the coach's tenure the team always seemed a yard or two off the pace.

A first-ever defeat to Argentina followed later that year in Salta, which started a sequence in which the Boks lost seven of the eight Tests that remained that year. It also included an ignominious first-ever defeat to Italy in Florence, but earlier in the year their old foe the All Blacks put 57 on them on home soil, hitherto arguably the Green and Gold's darkest hour.

There was a hint of optimism as the Boks started the following year with a five-match winning run against France and Argentina before they drew with the Wallabies in Perth. But their 57–0 defeat at the hands of the All Blacks in Albany was their nadir and a sobering reminder of how far they'd fallen behind the game's trendsetters. Even wins over France and Italy could not gloss over the dispiriting defeat against Ireland in Dublin and end-of-year Test loss against Wales in Cardiff.

After that Test Coetzee was asked in the press conference if he expected to still be the Springbok coach when England were due to visit South Africa in June the following year. He reminded them that he had a contract until 2019.

However, as he left the press conference room in the bowels of the Principality Stadium, I cornered Coetzee along with another South African journalist. Amid growing pressure back home for him to do so, he was confronted with the question: "Are you throwing in the towel?"

His parting words to us before he closed a passage door behind him were: "Who, me? You know me."

The door did, however, close on Coetzee as that Test proved to be his last in charge of the Springboks.

You had to feel for him. He agreed to coach the Boks with one arm tied to his back. He started late, he didn't always have the coaching back-up, couldn't select from a player pool as deep as is currently the case, and frankly he was at times undermined.

The following year Rassie Erasmus came to the Bok job endowed with infinitely more resources and technical expertise to set in motion a turn-around strategy. His brief was not just to make the Boks competitive in the short term but to set the building blocks in place that would give the team a realistic chance of winning the 2023 RWC in France. As director of rugby, he had a deeply reassuring seven-year contract.

Although the Boks faltered in their manic first outing under Erasmus in Washington in 2018, he had bigger fish to fry the following week. He rested several key players for the start of their three-Test series against England at Ellis Park and must have been mightily relieved to see his team prevail 42–39.

Picking his battles by carefully deploying his playing resources has become a hallmark of the Erasmus era. By casting his selection net wide, he has not only increased the depth of his talent pool, but has also, mostly, met transformation targets, which are inextricably linked to Springbok coaches' terms of employment.

When the RWC squad was announced in August, Erasmus had a dozen or so players of colour, a little short of the 50 per cent benchmark SA Rugby had hoped for. A little deviously, however, they set targets that are reviewed at the end of each year. By then, however, the coach – through his alignment camps in 2018 and 2019 – had exposed around 50 of the country's top players to his blueprint and what he expected from them.

There has been greater clarity in the way in which the Boks have gone about their business, much of it owed to the transparent way Erasmus has conducted his affairs with players and even the media.

One of his objectives has been to get everyone on the same page. Even before the RWC squad was announced, most pundits more or less knew the identity of the players due to travel to Japan.

Armed with what he believes is a bullet-proof blueprint and a healthy mix of youth and experience (14 survivors from the previous RWC), Erasmus boarded a jet bound for Singapore and then Tokyo much emboldened.

Epilogue

Japan and its Wonderfully Wild World Cup

In 2019, World Rugby brought the RWC to Asia for the first time, a gloriously generous leap into a not yet fully explored frontier. Some frowned upon the decision, a lot more were curious, while others felt they absolutely had to be part of it.

Japan is a place of wonder. Here you're drawn from your comfort zone, but at times firmly swept to a space of greater comfort. Japan perplexes, and it pleasures. It confuses, confounds, and it confronts our Western conformity with all manner of craziness, yet leaves you with common-sense clarity.

Even going to the toilet is an experience that takes a little adjusting to in Japan. Never mind the etiquette, just knowing which button to press can be a leap into the unknown. Bidet-style toilets have been installed in more than 80 per cent of households. The features include anal hygiene, bidet washing, seat warming and deodorising. Some toilets have as many as 38 buttons with a liquid crystal display.

Little wonder that one senior member of the Springbok coaching group got it wrong, or so he told us, by pressing the button for the bidet option. "Daai ding spuit my ballas sopnat," (that spurt really wet my balls) he told us amid raucous laughter.

Whether it is the way you travel around, how those close to you struggle to adjust, how you experience the food, being confronted with both ancient and modern, how the team you have been writing about for more than two decades has to think out of the Boks, Japan is one wild ride.

On the move, even if it's in the wrong direction

The mad dash for my connecting flight from Hong Kong to Tokyo was a portent of what was to come. The trip to Tokyo from Johannesburg was as short as it could possibly be when you consider that there are no direct flights from South Africa to Japan. This was going to be a RWC that requires lots of rapid movement. It was going to be a RWC defined by where you are positioned relative to the clock.

There are clear obstacles though. The language barrier makes navigating Japan daringly adventurous at times. When you ask for guidance you have to make sure of spelling and pronunciation. Even rail officials get it wrong, and most of the time those who are assigned to help do their best but on the odd occasion, particularly at busy train stations, those in uniform can be brusque.

Some member of the media travelling to a Springbok press conference found himself on a glorious misadventure one Friday. Although the team had been staying in Nagoya in preparation for their match against Namibia, the game was scheduled to be played in the city of Toyota, 53 kilometres to the east.

We had made Google enquiries and had found a route but in seeking clarity about the platform we should be boarding from, a Japan Rail employee noticed our rail passes and gave us different directions. After 20 minutes on a high-speed train we disembarked, made our way out of the station and did a Google search for the location of the stadium. We were aghast to find it 62 kilometres away to the northwest – we had been given directions to a platform for a train heading for Toyohashi and not our intended destination Toyotashi station.

On another occasion I tried to locate a particular bus outside Shin-Kobe and not Kobe station. Adjacent stations Kikugawa and Kakegawa also served to scramble the brain.

One writer, who has been on a number of tours, had no idea that Tokyo has two major international airports. The distance between Narita and Haneda is 76 kilometres, which can seriously impact your journey, especially when you are lugging a giant suitcase, or two.

Taxi drivers in Japan tend to be mature gentlemen, in every sense. They don't say much but neither do they take any nonsense. As I was leaving Omaezaki one bright sunny morning my quite elderly taxi driver shook his head while waving his finger animatedly at my preferred method of payment. I had no cash and he wasn't prepared to take the cash card I had been using to pay for all my previous taxi trips. There was a bit of to-ing and fro-ing and only after I mentioned a 7-Eleven did he understand I was in need of an ATM. We went our separate ways shaking our heads.

Public transport is next level. Even hotel shuttles run bang on time. In Kobe I was soon haunted by The Beatles' "Here Comes the Sun", which played on loop on the 20-minute shuttle ride from my hotel located in the port to Sannomiya station. Every day, on every ride, before the driver engaged second gear, an instrumental version of the song would kick in over the PA system. I love The Beatles but how those bus drivers did not feel the urge to drive off the end of the pier was beyond me. It is not of your choosing, but on almost every tour there's a song that gets stuck in your head. "Here Comes the Sun" was not what I had hoped for and I felt like Bill Murray in *Groundhog Day* every time I boarded that bus.

If the buses are on time, the bullet train – or Shinkansen – is an engineering marvel. Conceptualised at a time the jet engine took passengers higher, further and faster, the bullet train's ability not just to link major metropolitan areas but to get passengers into the heart of the city proved a game changer.

Travelling at speeds of just under 300 kilometres per hour, bullet trains are designed to link the business hubs of Tokyo and Osaka. The Nozomi, the fastest bullet train, completes the 506 kilometres between Japan's two biggest cities in two-and-a-half hours. Since its inception in the mid-1960s the network has been extended and now links the northeastern tip of the main island of Honshu with Kyushu way to the southwest.

Watching Japan's countryside blur by on a bullet train is a true delight.

Bad company, maybe not

On long tours you'll find, after a while, that the days tick over almost imperceptibly. One moment you're perfectly aware that you've been gone for two of the seven weeks on the road, and suddenly you're hit with the realisation that you've passed the halfway mark.

Your travel companions can have a huge impact on how you experience a country. Fortunately, some of us have been travelling together for a while – one hack on this tour was even with me at the 1999 RWC.

Things are never dull among the travelling troupe. On this trip we had one writer particularly devoted to porn. When the Boks toured more frequently in the 1990s he would often accompany the team. South Africans, who were in many ways shielded from the ways of the world back then, were often shocked at what was readily available on their travels. And so it was with porn for this writer. He would spend hours in his room accessing late-night channels on his television. And on one trip he actually went down to reception to complain about what he deemed a substandard offering on the hotel's adult-entertainment bouquet. A week later, in a different city, a more satisfactory porn menu was on offer, but the problem was that his wife had by then joined him, which pretty much put paid to his viewing pleasure.

The same writer, although a seasoned traveller, would work himself into a froth over something others wouldn't give a second thought. In Japan he kept complaining about how high his hotel room was and how disconcerting that was. High-rise buildings tend to sway a little in the wind, but he was more concerned about how gravity would impact him should, say, an earthquake bring down the establishment.

At the opposite end of the scale was a young reporter on his first Springbok tour who, we found, is easily spooked. In Omaezaki, with its lush coastal vegetation, we encountered a particular type of spider that was quite industrious in spinning its web. When you go for a run, for instance, you will almost certainly bring some of the spider's dwelling back to your room.

Just thinking of the large but harmless (I think) spider gave this reporter the creeps. He was also on high alert at the prospect of an earthquake. The fact that our hotel in Omaezaki was alongside a decommissioned nuclear power station didn't sit easy with him either. He needed no reminding of what happened at Fukushima in 2011 when an earthquake and resultant tsunami caused a nuclear meltdown.

Omaezaki is located in an earthquake zone and so high are the odds on a major quake striking the area that the plant was decommissioned following the Fukushima disaster in 2011. The decommissioned power plant is located five kilometres from where the Springboks stayed but was visible from their hillside retreat.

One morning, at exactly 2.15, a tremor shook me awake. My bed swayed sideways. There was nothing violent about the tremor – in fact, the short shake almost rocked me to sleep. At breakfast the next morning I asked whether anyone had felt the tremor. The young reporter's jaw dropped.

"There was a tremor?" he asked with eyes wide. He had not felt it, but added, "I would've kakked myself!"

Another reporter who was actually awake at that hour didn't feel a thing.

The tremor registered 4.1 on the Richter scale, so was a full seismic event.

As if the week the Boks spent in Omaezaki wasn't eventful enough, not-so-friendly neighbours North Korea resumed hostilities by firing a ballistic missile into the Sea of Japan.

Just to spook the young reporter further we made up a story of a Japanese tokoloshe, the Terrorgochi, that visits you when you're in your deepest sleep. This time he almost did "kak" himself.

Bokking the trend

After all their pre-tournament exertions, the Boks did their final preparations east of the megalopolis in Tokyo Bay. Their hotel, as luck would have it, was right next to Disneyworld, which meant that hotels in the Bay area are family orientated, with kids running in – if not ruling – lobbies.

Tired of writing in my room I found a spot in the hotel's lounge area adjacent to reception. A six-year-old and his toddler sister would run laps around the area, throwing and chasing after a small toy. Eventually he spotted me, his laps bringing him in an ever-widening orbit towards me. On one lap he suddenly stopped and seated himself next to me. "Kanichiwa!" he said mischievously, looking down at his toy.

I replied, and he smiled, got up and started a fresh lap. The process repeated itself four times until a couple, to my grateful surprise, finally decided to resume their parental duties.

One day the Boks' proximity to Disneyworld spilled over in a press conference. Tendai "Beast" Mtawarira blushed like a pubescent teen when continually pressed on whether he had visited the Disney theme park. Beast kept answering "no" and the journalist afterwards admitted to us, his colleagues back at the office wanted him to elecit a Beast-and-Disney headline from Tendai.

In fact, the Springboks' choice of hotels on this trip raised a few eyebrows. In Omaezaki, in the Shizuoka Prefecture, they stayed at an exclusive golf resort. The hotel was located on a hillside about five kilometres from the nearest town with great vistas of the Pacific Ocean in the distance; coach Rassie Erasmus liked the hotel because it was secluded; his players not so much – there were no distractions for them.

The sleepy town we shared with the Boks looks rather like Sedgefield in the Southern Cape on one side of the main drag and the Cape Town suburb of Lakeside on the other. It didn't have much by way of restaurant options, but at least there was a McDonald's. This meant that we often bumped into Springbok coaching staff and management in the few restaurants dotted around town. On one occasion, in a splendid Nepalese curry house, the only patrons in the place were members of the Bok team or South African media.

Erasmus could not get quite the same seclusion in Kobe, so he settled for a hotel on an island. Japan's population is cramped into only 20 per cent of its landmass; they don't have many navigable rivers and the ubiquitous mountainous terrain has helped contribute to high population density on its southern coastline. The result is that Kobe, hemmed in by the Pacific Ocean in the south and craggy mountains to the north, has been running out of space for some time, which is why they started reclaiming land from the sea in the 1960s. On one such island, Rokkō, the Boks dropped anchor for a week before they moved to Tokyo for the knock-out stages.

What they were perhaps unaware of when they made their choice of hotel is that reclaimed land is far more susceptible to earthquakes – in fact, earthquakes that last for, say, 20 to 30 seconds on the mainland can rattle on for between two and three minutes on the reclaimed land.

Trouble stirring

Soon after arriving in Japan, there's an elephant in the room. No, a giraffe. Actually, no, he's not even in the room.

Eben Etzebeth, that gloriously strapping and muscular behemoth, had been the talk of the town back home for allegedly being part of a late-night (early-morning) fracas that left at least one man injured. Coupled with that, there was also the accusation that he hurled racial slurs. Naturally, this had woke folk frothing at the mouth but if even half of what was suggested was true, then the player's presence in a Springbok RWC squad would be deeply undesirable.

However, the truism "innocent until proven guilty" was the defence used by the Boks, and Rassie Erasmus – Springbok coach, SA Rugby director and the man who opted to select Etzebeth despite the allegations before the squad was officially unveiled – stuck to his guns. He kept telling the media that he knows Etzebeth. In fact, he made the point once during the RWC that he was part of the decision-making process that saw Etzebeth sign for the Stormers as a youngster. He made the point that the player came from "a difficult background". He had asked Etzebeth about the incident and the player had denied any culpability.

Erasmus's decision to include the player who was seen as central to their challenge for the RWC also meant that they would have to do everything to keep him from the glare of the media. Naturally, we had access to a member of the coaching set-up and at least four players for most days of the week. When I, a little facetiously, reminded the media manager that they would soon run out of players and that Etzebeth would have to be next, he grinned and walked away. The party line was that Etzebeth was off limits.

Our view, though, was that, guilty or not, you can't have a player at the RWC and not present him for interviews. No top table appearances, no mixed zone and certainly no one-on-ones. In fact, asking for one-on-ones at this RWC was like asking permission to urinate on Doc Danie Craven's grave. We were told that the decision to declare Etzebeth off limits was an SA Rugby decision, but when I asked Mark Alexander, the president of the organisation, if this was their decision, he denied it – which basically means it was a decision made by the coach, presumably in consultation with their head of communications.

Boks on course despite the typhoon

The Springboks lose their much-anticipated RWC opener against the All Blacks. Although they make a proper fist of it, they also prove a little hamfisted in attack. They squander several scoring opportunities and let the All Blacks off the hook in a 23–13 defeat.

They also lose tighthead prop Trevor Nyakane to injury. The sight of Nyakane hobbling off is a little disconcerting but thankfully the Boks are well stocked in the prop department. The Boks are devastated but there is no time to mope. They have to get going.

Coach Rassie Erasmus stresses that their match against Italy has become a must-win affair. The Boks are supposed to have the measure of Namibia and Canada in their pool, but the Azzurri might be a tough nut to crack.

Next, though, it's off to Nagoya where the Boks will prepare for their match against Namibia. They are expected to win at a canter and the game gives Erasmus the opportunity to rest some star players.

In Nagoya, the Boks' hotel is within walking distance of other hotels dotted around the CBD, which also means players and coaches are more likely to bump into journalists. And there is at least one semi-awkward moment when some players walk in on a few scribes at a Hooters outlet. For the bulk of them, instead of a handshake, the distant, knowing nod of the head is the order of the day. The scribes are there to watch a match involving Ireland and, we believe, Scotland.

From the moment Ireland wins their RWC opening match against Scotland they have the Boks in their crosshairs. They had come into the tournament as the top ranked team in the world, and their many followers – including some in their media contingent – have accepted that the Springboks will be their quarter-final opponents. Some Irish reporters start muscling in on Bok press conferences, interrogating Erasmus about the things he learnt when he was at Munster. They are obsessed with the fact that Erasmus and his coaching staff know more about Ireland than they know about the Boks. The Irish hacks are becoming a nuisance but then Ireland go and lose to Japan. They stop coming to the Bok pressers.

On match day the Boks romp home 57–3 and although they weren't at their best it is mission accomplished. Besides, the win means that they are off the mark. Erasmus talks up Italy, but we don't buy it. They haven't won a game in the Six Nations since 2015. Yes, they did beat the Boks in 2016, but this is a very different Springbok team. Perhaps it's the occasion more than the opposition that has Erasmus concerned. The Boks can't afford to lose the game because the loser will almost certainly fail to qualify for the next round.

Italy goes into the match having had eight days to prepare while the Boks have had half that time to ready themselves. It doesn't show, however, because the Boks start like a house on fire. Some slick handling and incisive running leaves the Azzurri clutching thin air as the Boks put the match beyond the reach of the Italians in the first half. They are unable to sustain that momentum in the second because the greasy ball becomes increasingly difficult to handle, but the Boks nevertheless go on to win 49–3 and effectively qualify for the knock-out stages at the expense of Italy.

The Boks have in the meantime also lost centre Jesse Kriel to injury. He is said to have sustained a slight bump on his hamstring against New Zealand and while he is expected to make a quick recovery he has aggravated the injury and has to go home.

Kriel is replaced by the exciting utility back Damian Willemse who would have been part of the squad had injury not initially robbed him a place. He comes straight into the team at fullback for the Boks' last pool match against Canada in Kobe.

Kobe, I'm sad to say, is mostly remembered for the devastating earthquake that took place in January 1995. The quake registered 6.9 on the Richter scale, with up to 6 434 people perishing in the disaster. The place has, however, risen from those ruins. They warm easily to visitors. They also have an obsession with beef. Kobe beef, although expensive, with some servings going up to R8 700, is widely accessible in the town. There are different grades, though, which means prices fluctuate wildly.

I experienced Kobe beef for the first time in Sydney during the 2003 RWC so I am quite keen to try it again. Then we receive news that the local tourism authority wants to take us on a mini junket that includes lunch, incorporating Kobe beef. This basically involves a short boat cruise, followed by a 40-minute journey on a bus through the mountains that guard the north of the city and on to Arima Onsen, one of the oldest spa resorts in Japan.

Spending 45 minutes in the three different baths on offer is just what the doctor ordered. The Boks smash Canada 66–7 and are really annoyed that they conceded a try. It is only the third they had conceded in the tournament but now they have a marathon 12-day break before their quarter-final.

They said it

Unsurprisingly, England coach Eddie Jones was in fine form in front of the microphones at the RWC. Earlier in the year he had raised eyebrows in Japan for referring to flankers Tom Curry and Sam Underhill as "kamikaze kids". The word "kamikaze" is sensitive in Japan because it refers to pilots who flew aircraft into Allied ships in suicide missions during World War II, but after England's game against Tonga during the RWC, a Japanese reporter got an opportunity to seek clarification from Jones.

"The meaning of 'kamikaze kids' is those two guys, Curry and Underhill, they just rip and tear," Jones said. "They've got no care for their bodies and they lead the way in terms of our defensive effort."

Then, in the build-up to the game against the United States, Jones opined that the Americans would "play like 15 Donald Trumps". Asked to explain, he said, "They'll give everything. They're gonna come out guns blazing."

After England's first game against Tonga on Japan's northern Hokkaido island, Jones reckoned it would be special to take rugby to a region unfamiliar with the game. Then, he added, Hokkaido was "closer to Russia than you probably want to be". In that moment it perhaps escaped him that Russia was also playing in the RWC.

On the nose injury Owen Farrell suffered against the United States, Jones was a little graphic. "He's missing part of his nose, which is unfortunate. But he's married, he's got a child and he's not looking for any young lass in Kobe tonight so he'll be okay."

At one point a Zimbabwean-born journalist who calls South Africa home asked Jones whether the Tier 2 nations were getting a raw deal at the RWC. They had shorter turn-around times for their matches and they were generally treated like second-class citizens in the world of rugby.

"Springbok!" Jones said to the reporter, thinking he had nailed his nationality. "Are you the younger or the older brother? Tier 2 teams are like the younger brother. No matter what you give them, they're never happy."

Australia coach Michael Cheika also got in to the act. "He has a few more grey hairs than he did in the past. He thinks they make him look more distinguished. I think they just make him look older. He has that, as they say in French, *je ne sais quoi*," said Cheika of the grizzled Adam Ashley-Cooper.

Early in the tournament the high humidity made the ball very difficult to handle. Coaches had to find different ways to prepare their players for this challenge. That explains why this strange question was asked during a press conference. "Guys, I heard that Warren Gatland [the Wales coach] has been putting baby oil on his ball … I mean his rugby balls."

Horrible Hagibis

I have always been morbidly fascinated by disasters, natural or otherwise. When the spectre of super typhoon Hagibis starts looming large I feel the urge to leave Kobe. It will only be brushed by the typhoon's outer reaches – the real action is going to be in Tokyo and, as it turns out, I'm due to leave for the capital the morning of the typhoon's arrival. Public transport will, however, grind to a halt so I'll need to move early. I weigh up my options. Do I wait it out, or do I press on to Tokyo?

There are minor financial implications. Should I stay I will have to book an extra night in Kobe and cough up for a pricey one-way rail ticket on the bullet train as my rail pass is due to expire.

The typhoon has a huge impact.

In the end, at least 78 lives are lost, with some still unaccounted for. Before it hits, authorities issue a general warning: "Typhoon Hagibis is on track to make landfall in Japan on Saturday, 12 October, tracking east through Sunday, 13 October. Wide areas across eastern, western and northern Japan will be affected by strong winds as well as torrential and sustained heavy rain that bring the risk of floods and landslide. Storm surges are expected across the coast of eastern Japan on Saturday and Sunday.

"According to the Japan Meteorological Agency, this typhoon is anticipated to be the most powerful storm of the year, so be prepared and stay safe. Remain indoors, check typhoon-related updates regularly and follow the advice of local authorities including any evacuation orders and ensure you have basic food provisions. Keep travel documents and essential medication with you in case you have to move at short notice and let family and friends in your home country know you are safe."

Hagibis impacts the tournament dramatically. On the grounds of public safety, three matches are cancelled: England and France, New Zealand and Italy, and Namibia and Canada. There is also the prospect of Japan's last pool match against Scotland being called off.

It causes a storm. Scotland remonstrate and threaten legal action because they need to win this match in order to progress to the next round. Japan would go through if the match was called off, but their coach Jamie Joseph decides to set the record straight.

"We have worked very hard to get the team to where it is," says Joseph. "This team has been in camp for the last 240 days. While the majority of the players are professionals with company-based teams, as a rugby team, Japan is amateur. Other than $100 a day [R1 495 expense allowance], no one gets paid for being in camp. I will let you guys do the maths and make comparisons with other teams.

"Everyone in our camp, players and staff, want to play the match against Scotland. We all want to earn the right to be considered one of the elite teams in the world. It is important for us to wake up on Monday and understand we are a worthy top eight team or not good enough. My team is motivated by achieving something that is great, not avoiding an embarrassment."

In the end that match is indeed played and it is a truly memorable one. When Italy's match against New Zealand is cancelled it robs captain Sergio Parisse – who had played 142 times for his country – a proper opportunity to depart the stage. "It is difficult to know that we won't have the chance to play a match against one of the great teams. If New Zealand needed four or five points against us it would not have been cancelled," said Parisse.

"It is ridiculous that a decision of this nature has been made because it isn't like the fans arrived yesterday. It is ridiculous that there was no Plan B, because it isn't news that typhoons hit Japan.

"Sure, everyone might think that Italy versus New Zealand being cancelled counts for nothing because we'd have lost anyway, but we deserved to be respected as a team.

"We had the chance to play in a big stadium, against a great team. The alternative is Plan B. When you organise a World Cup you should have one in place. Sure, if Italy and New Zealand decide they don't want to play, then fine but, as I said before, if New Zealand needed the points, it wouldn't have been cancelled."

The storm terrorises Tokyo and causes vast flooding in low lying areas on Japan's southern coastline. Storm surges also wreak havoc.

In the end I decide to stay in Kobe and travel to Tokyo on the Sunday. I have to buy a new ticket but the important thing is that the rail network is up and running. Japan's ability to get up after being punched to a pulp never ceases to amaze.

As I'm typing, the "Hikari" Shinkansen bullet train is steaming towards Tokyo at great speed. It would have covered the 532 kilometres between Kobe and Tokyo in a shade over three hours.

It is at Tokyo station where this train terminates, and so does this book.

Acknowledgements

WHERE I GREW UP dreams are rarely realised. Many parents might have found my devotion to sport deeply troubling, so I owe a huge amount of gratitude to my deceased parents, Olga and Patrick, who indulged my obsessions and allowed me to simply be. That helped set me on a path to write, watch sport and travel and I could not have asked for more.

My journey has taken me to more than 150 Tests and has culminated in *Winging It: On tour with the Boks* and although I was initially reluctant to write a book about my travels (I figured who on earth would be interested?) persuasive publisher Nadia Goetham not to mention my partner, Marcelle Gordon, eventually prevailed upon me to document some of those experiences. Nadia's commitment and dedication to this cause has been quite staggering.

This book would not be possible without the journos, coaches and players, my fellow passengers on this journey. It is mostly about the journos, however, and to my brothers and compadres – among them Vata Ngobeni, Brenden Nel, Gavin Rich, Simnikiwe Xabanisa, Jon Cardinelli, Ken Borland, Kevin McCallum, Gerald Imray, Louis de Villiers and Mike

Greenaway, the folk with whom I share these experiences – I owe you a beer.

To Xola Ntshinga, Owen Nkumane, Gcobani Bobo, Naas Botha, Joel Stransky, Natalie Germanos, Neil Andrews and Jean de Villiers who gave so generously of their time, I say thank you.

A final word of thanks to Marcelle, and our four-legged housemates Jackson and Jemima. Marcelle is endowed with many fine virtues but her patience and understanding throughout this project, and – to be fair – well before, has proved a source of immense comfort and inspiration. These experiences may well have been less enjoyable had it not been for the selfless dedication of my greatest fan. I dedicate this to you.

上陸許可(再)
17. SEP . 2019
NARITA(2)
入国審査官・日本国

1569